The *Holiday* Guide to
PARIS

Prepared with the cooperation of the editors of HOLIDAY magazine.

RANDOM HOUSE 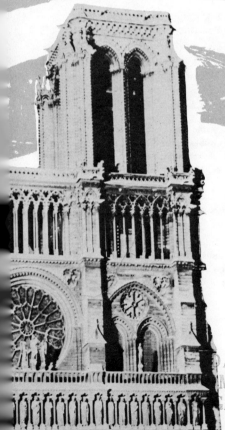 NEW YORK

Photographs courtesy of
the French Government Tourist Office

Copyright © 1960, 1962, 1964, 1966, 1968, 1971, 1973, 1976
by The Curtis Publishing Company

Library of Congress Cataloging in Publication Data
Main entry under title:

The Holiday guide to Paris.

(The Holiday magazine travel guide series ; 4)
Previous editions published under title: Paris.
Includes index.
1. Paris—Description—1975-   —Guide-books.
I. Holiday. II. Series.
    DC708.P27 1976   914.4′36′0483   75–31763
               ISBN 0–394–73200–6

Manufactured in the United States of America
9 8 7 6 5 4 3 2
Revised Edition

CONTENTS

CHAPTER *1*

You probably couldn't start much of a quarrel anywhere by saying that Paris is the most glorious city in the world. The reason for such general agreement is simple: other cities may have one or two features that Paris lacks, but this completely enthralling metropolis has qualities that no other urban area even approaches.

Most of all, there are the moods of Paris, as varied as the life of the city itself. Each quarter has a life and mood of its own, as if they were different cities and possessed different personalities. Some visitors will prefer the mood of Paris that is set by the Cathedral of Notre Dame on the Ile de la Cité, the historical nucleus of the city; others will prefer that set by the Seine as it flows through the heart of the city, beneath the many arched bridges, past the quiet Ile Saint Louis with its ancient dignified mansions, by the gardens of the Tuileries and of the Palais de Chaillot, and out past Auteuil.

The Seine divides Paris into Right and Left Banks. The Left Bank, *la rive gauche,* contains the Latin Quarter with the Sorbonne and the French Academy—for centuries the focal point of the intellectual activity of France; there, too, is the aristocratic Faubourg St. Germain, the artistic quarter of Montparnasse, and the Eiffel Tower. On the opposite side of the Seine are the fashionable hotels and shops, the great boulevards, the Champs-Elysées, and the Louvre. Whether your mood be brisk or leisurely, whether you crave luxury or simplicity, you will find your desire somewhere in Paris.

In all the important things you ask of a city, Paris gives at least a double measure, and it will be offered with grace. Every conceivable appetite can be satisfied here, and, because this is Paris, the satisfaction is given without a trace of reproach. Unless you choose to be-

The Eiffel Tower is the symbol of the city

come actively involved in politics, you will find it difficult to arouse the indignation of the Parisians, for they surpass all other people at understanding the foibles of the human being.

Culturally, Paris is one of the centers of the world. Her theaters, with offerings ranging from the great classic works of Corneille and Racine to the contemporary masterpieces of Ionesco and Beckett, are as stimulating as any in the world. Her concert halls are both numerous and varied in their selection of recitals. And so well known is the Parisian concern with painting and sculpture that it is almost unnecessary to talk about her galleries and museums. Paris was the fountainhead of the new cinema in the fifties and still occupies a prominent position in the art.

For appetites somewhat less lofty, the entertainment offered by the Paris night clubs may be earthy, but only occasionally is it lascivious. Her restaurants are legendary—it is hardly news that among them you will find the best in the world—and they are nearly as plentiful and varied as the bars and cafés that are found on every corner. And the French, aware of the virtues of an appeal to the eye, present your food as they present their city—magnificently. The United States learned the arts of packaging from the French.

If there were a fair criticism of Paris, it would have to be that there is too much for a visitor to absorb in the short time usually afforded to him. Where to begin?

The marvelous parks and gardens that grace this most beautifully planned of all the world's cities; the charming walks along the Seine, lined with trees and open-air bookstalls; the proud monuments to days of grandeur; the fabulous art treasures; the magnificent boulevards and the little narrow side streets veering crazily off in all directions—all are things that must be seen. Even the odors of the city are vivid. The garlic and perfume of the Métro—Paris' superb subway system—the sweet, fresh smell of flowers from the myriad gardens and flower stalls. And surely the most typical—and least expensive—of Parisian pleasures is the open-air café. To a Frenchman, the streets and cafés of Paris are his second home, and a seat on the terrace of a lively café will give you a wonderful view of the spirited life that goes on there. It was at the Left Bank café, Deux Magots that Sartre and Simone de Beauvoir talked about and built Existentialism after the war; in Latin Quarter cafés, students started the 1968 general strike; and at the famous Café de la Paix, on the Right Bank, lovers and friends, and even chic shoppers, have sipped *café* for generations.

The city is full of associations, for it is the most painted and photographed place on earth. The Eiffel Tower is more than a relic of the Exposition of 1889; it is the symbol of the city. There are other symbols, too—Notre Dame . . . Les Invalides, where the great Napoleon lies in his sumptuous tomb . . . the Luxembourg Gardens, which belong to the children of Paris and to Sorbonne students . . . the Arc de

Triomphe and the Arc de Triomphe du Carrousel . . . the Champs-Elysées, where you sit and make bets about how many people you know will pass by . . . Père Lachaise, that most extraordinary of cemeteries . . . the Bois de Boulogne where you may ride in a fiacre or dine under the trees, or the smaller Bois de Vincennes with its splendid zoo . . . the Ritz on the Place Vendôme, where so many Americans have hidden out from themselves or from Prohibition . . . the Sainte Chapelle, gothic and magnificent, and a modern monument, the UNESCO building . . . the magnificent brooding Louvre where you must at least pay your respects to Mona Lisa and Winged Victory . . . the elegance of l'Opéra on an opening night . . . the Rue St. Honoré, the Rue de Rivoli, and the Rue de la Paix, where you can spend a lifetime's savings in an afternoon—these are only a few of the symbols of Paris.

Though you may never have considered it, Paris happened to you long before you ever got here. Western civilization is full of what Paris has been exporting for so many years—not only clothes and perfumes, fine food, and art, but something perhaps best described as the Parisian spirit: elegance, taste, relaxation, enchantment. Until quite recently, after all, before the world gave up good manners and tact and graciousness, it was to Paris that young people were sent to learn these graces. And before that, in the Middle Ages, it was to Paris, to the Sorbonne, the western world's center of learning, that men came to learn everything else as well.

There is another story about Paris and another general. When the Germans were getting ready to evacuate the capital, the command came from Hitler to blow up the city. But the commanding general, von Choltitz, disobeyed the order. He could not bear, he said, to go down in history as the man who had destroyed Paris.

More than any other single quality that distinguishes Paris—more than its lively and charming people, its broad avenues lined with plane and chestnut trees, its monuments and churches—is what the French call "le cadre"—the presentation, the frame, of their city. Notice how artistically the displays in the luxury shop windows are prepared, as if they were part of an art exhibition. Even the little flower-vendor arranges her stall with infallible taste. This visual concern has attained a new impetus under the Fifth Republic. Because of a 1961 law requiring the cleaning of building façades every ten years, you may be surprised to discover that the city's celebrated greys have been restored to their original pinks, creams, yellows and whites. Many parts of town are already getting their second "face lifting," for no one loves Paris more than the Parisian himself; he wants you to see his adored city in the happiest possible light. And the success of his effort is what makes Paris the loveliest city on earth.

CHAPTER 2

Paris is a relatively modern city compared to Rome or London, and its history, so far as political significance is attached to it, goes back only about a thousand years. But a millennium is long enough for some rather firm traditions to be established. And Paris has been the capital of France—culturally—to a degree that neither Rome nor London has enjoyed in Italy or England. Its influence has not lessened politically, historically or economically, since the 10th century, when it really came into existence as a city of importance.

The cultural tradition of Paris, of course, is the one most familiar to the visitor—and properly so, since this is the quality that makes Paris so beguiling. But from the historical standpoint, the tradition of political awareness and concern is of paramount importance. Cosmopolitan, urbane, worldly—all are adjectives you may safely apply to Paris. But if this leads you to infer that Paris is indifferent to affairs of state, you are astonishingly mistaken. However languidly the Parisian may regard matters that attract considerable attention in other cities, he is certain to react to politics with almost appalling vigor, and regardless of what the issue may be, he will have ideas of his own that differ so much from those of his neighbors that you may conclude that he is more an advocate of anarchy than of systematic government. Over the centuries, this political excitability of Parisians has been a decisive factor in the rise and fall of governments.

The origins of the French capital are obscure. There is little doubt that the Celtic tribes who settled in northern France before the Roman conquest established a fishing community on what is now known as the Ile de la Cité. But it was Caesar's legions who designated this town as Lutetia of the Parisii (the name of the Gallic in-

The Place de la Concorde at night—Paris' most beautiful square

habitants), which was later contracted to its present form. However, the great history of the city lay far in the future. Under the Romans, Paris became a river trading center, but not nearly as important as the cities of Lyon or Arles to the south.

Indeed, it was not until the 5th-century triumph of the Franks—first over Attila the Hun at Troyes, and later over their allies, the Visigoths—that Paris attained any real significance, and this was short lived. Clovis, a Frankish barbarian who assumed the rule of Rome by force and shrewdly adopted the Christian religion, built a crude fortress where the palace of the Emperor Julian the Apostate had stood on the Ile de la Cité, and made Paris his capital. Thus the Ile de la Cité became known as the Island of the Franks, and thus the region around Paris derived its eventual name of Ile de France.

Charlemagne established his capital at Aix-la-Chapelle (Aachen in modern Germany) at the end of the 8th century, and for the next 150 years, Paris was neglected by history, though hardly by the Viking barbarians, who repeatedly voyaged up the Seine from the English Channel and attacked the town.

When Hugues Capet came to the throne in 987, he chose Paris for his capital. He was the first of a line which, with its collateral descendants, ruled France for nearly a thousand years. The islands on the Seine were reasonably easy to defend; the climate was salubrious, and the location central. From time to time Capet's heirs would prefer the quiet beauty of the Loire valley and move the entire court to Blois or Chambord, but from the outset of the Capetian dynasty Paris remained the true capital. There are some relics from earlier days—the Roman baths, which are now part of the Musée de Cluny, the Arena near the Jardin des Plantes, the catacombs of Montparnasse—and there is the tradition of St. Denis who, after being decapitated for refusing to worship at the Roman temple of Mercury on Montmartre, is said to have walked five miles from the scene of his execution, his head tucked beneath his arm, to the suburb that now bears his name, where he was buried. But it was the Capets who built the Paris we recognize today.

History, it is true, was on the side of the Capet monarchs; but they helped it along. The barbarian invasions, which had been blocked with increasing effectiveness by the development of fortifications capable of resisting siege, drew to a close in the 10th century. The individual feudal strongholds, no longer of much use for military purposes, gave way to towns. Trade was resumed and with it, coinage; the Capets became the bankers of France, and Paris became the city to which all large-scale borrowers were compelled to come. Moreover, the descendants of Hugues Capet began to accumulate property—in their own name, which they conceived to be synonymous with that of the French nation.

With a strong monarchy at last a reality—though this reality was to be shattered later on—the growth of Paris was assured. The great

Ile de la Cité and Notre Dame

churches of Notre Dame and St. Martin-des-Champs were built, the
Louvre was begun, the streets were cobbled, the defensive ramparts
and watchtowers of les Chatelets were breached from within because
Paris was getting too big for its walls and gates. By the early 13th century, it had grown to be more than a trading center and the seat of
the monarchy, it had become the center of learning for northwestern
Europe. From Britain, from Holland and the German principalities,
students came to the Sorbonne—the great university on the Left
Bank of the Seine—to be educated in all that the Church, which
then controlled it, had managed to preserve of Roman knowledge,
in art, law, medicine, and theology.

In the 12th century Pierre Abélard—whose love for Héloise cost
him his manhood—had done his best to reconcile the arguments of
Plato and Aristotle, which had been rediscovered only a short time
before. with the doctrine that the Church must be taken on faith.
Thomas Aquinas, an Italian by birth, who nevertheless found recognition and understanding in the intellectual atmosphere of 13th century Paris, resolved the difficulty Abélard had propounded. St.
Thomas argued with brilliant simplicity that "Truth is one; hence
truth according to [scientific] knowledge and truth according to faith
must coincide." With a single phrase, he had legitimized the pursuit
of non-scriptural knowledge and had established for France the intellectual tradition that has endured to this day.

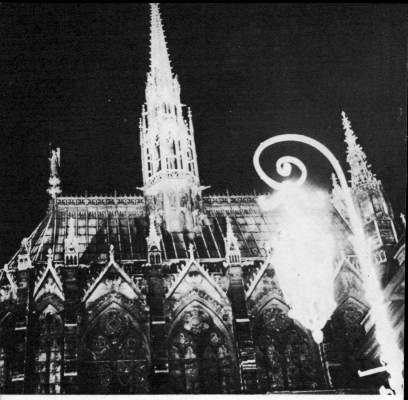

The exquisite Sainte Chapelle of Louis IX

Of the Capet kings, one especially contributed inestimably to the glory of Paris. He was Louis IX, Saint Louis, whose name is given to the little island next to the Ile de la Cité. It was this saintly king who was responsible for La Sainte Chapelle, surely one of the most beautiful Gothic buildings of Paris and of the world. But he was almost too good a man—he was too good to his enemies, especially—and his grandson, Philippe le Bel, had to undo many of Saint Louis' good deeds in order to preserve the kingdom.

By the middle of the 14th century, at the beginning of the Hundred Years War, France for the first time was truly a nation. She was forty times larger than she had been at the outset of the reign of the Capets. Paris, with more than a quarter of a million inhabitants, was the hub of all that was French, politically and artistically, culturally and intellectually. But the locusts were on the point of closing in.

When disaster struck, it came from all sides. The zenith of the monarchy—when the Papacy, as a result of a schism in the Church, was established at Avignon in southern France, and the Capets dominated Europe's confused arena of war and marriage—had passed. First the British, richer and better organized than the French (who hated to pay taxes even then and who resisted rule, though it was in

their interest not to), attacked. The question was possession of Aqui-
taine, and rule of Normandy—indeed, rule of all of France, for the
British, through the descendants of William the Conqueror, had what
might have appeared to be a legitimate claim to the French throne
after the death of the last Capet king. Then came the Plague—the
Black Death—which, in a single year, killed a third of France's
twenty-five million people. The combination of internal dissension,
external attack, plague, and famine was too much for the country.

In Paris, in the middle of the 14th century, there was an uprising
against the increased taxation needed for the war against Britain.
The monarchy, though powerful enough to suppress this small rebellion, could not withstand the strains of both war and dissension.
It didn't collapse; it almost withered away. It was left to Jeanne d'Arc
to save the throne and protect the nation from the weakness and in-
decision of a bankrupt and demoralized leadership. Where reason
and numerical superiority had failed, faith prevailed. It was a miracle. It was, in reality, two miracles: Jeanne first recaptured Orléans
from the British and then persuaded the weak and cowardly Dauphin
to be anointed king in the Cathedral at Reims. A third miracle was
needed, but Jeanne could not quite manage it. Paris also was in the
hands of Britain. Jeanne attempted to drive them out in 1430, but
this time she failed. Only six years later, after she had been burned
as a heretic, Paris at last was free. And within twenty years of her
death, France finally was completely evacuated of British troops,
largely as a result of her inspiration.

The period following the Hundred Years War saw the rebuilding
of the French kingdom. François I, the first important Valois monarch, who began his reign in 1515, brought back the stirring ideas of
the Renaissance from a military adventure in Italy. He retained the
services of that greatest of Renaissance figures, Leonardo da Vinci,
and of that greatest of goldsmiths, the rascally Cellini. François
Rabelais, whose ribald epic of Gargantua and Pantagruel found favor
at court, became the first French writer of importance and influenced
the work of the king's sister, Marguérite de Navarre, whose *Hepta-
meron* was only slightly less bawdy than Rabelais' own work.

François I founded the Collège de France in Paris; added to the
Louvre, and the Tuileries; and enlarged the Palais of Fontainebleau.
In other ways, though, François I was less than a great king; he was
unable to cope with the great issues of his day, especially that of religion. It would be convenient to say that the problem of religious faith
in Renaissance Europe was simply one of Protestantism versus Ca-
tholicism. But it was much more complicated than that, for within
each rival group factions were at work and, especially in France,
where the right of opposition was as important as wine or bread, the
divisions increased at an alarming rate, breaking out occasionally
into open warfare. And the question of religious toleration would not
be finally resolved until 1774.

The attitude of Paris on the religious issue was amply demonstrated when, after his accession to the throne in 1589, Henri IV—the first Bourbon king—was denied physical admission to the city until he foreswore his former Protestant faith in favor of the religion of Rome. The significance of this open rebellion against the royal authority was lost on Henri IV, who was neither a particularly subtle nor farsighted monarch. He saw no handwriting on the wall in these Parisian actions.

The issue of religion, however, was merely one of many that divided France. Despite the entrenchment of the monarchy and the final establishment of a France that had grown to a size resembling its modern boundaries, the nobility and the *haute bourgeoisie* were constantly ready to dispute the royal will. Henri IV dealt easily with everyone; placation was his way.

It was hardly the way with the prime minister of his successor, Louis XIII. Cardinal Richelieu, the "gray eminence," sought to reverse completely the pattern that Henri IV had set. By stern control of the courts of justice—he dictated the verdicts they would reach before the trials began—Richelieu enforced an absolute loyalty to the throne, something that had never before been achieved in France. The Cardinal paid a heavy price in popularity. The restless nobles demanded his dismissal, but Louis XIII depended on Richelieu, who was, in effect, the regent. Regardless of what the public thought of him, Cardinal Richelieu accomplished many things without which France would have been a good deal poorer. His creation of *L'Académie Française,* whose purpose was, and still is, to discuss and improve the French language, is responsible today for the fact that this language—among all contemporary tongues—lends itself best to real precision. He accorded a degree of independence and intellectual freedom to the French universities that they had not before possessed —and this tradition has been maintained through the ensuing centuries. It was under his patronage that the great classical age of literature flourished in Paris: this was the time of Descartes, the great mathematician and philosopher, and of Racine and Corneille, the epic poets of the French theater. Painters and architects too were given privileges and pensions that made their work possible. All this France owes to the influence of Richelieu. And it owes him, politically, an even greater debt: he unified the nation.

The almost simultaneous deaths of Richelieu and Louis XIII brought to the throne, in 1643, Louis XIV; he was five years old—too young to rule, but not too young to drink. His mother was named regent, and she turned to another Cardinal, Mazarin, to serve as her Richelieu. Mazarin's purpose was identical to that of his predecessor, but his methods were different and, to the French, more insidious. The fact that he was Italian, and had been exposed to the lessons in treachery offered by the Borgias and the Medicis, probably influenced Mazarin's thinking. No bother with the niceties of trials for him, he

Orangerie at Versailles

had his opponents murdered, preferably in the dark shadows of Paris streets from which there were plenty to choose, street-lighting being limited to a few boulevards. Compared to Mazarin, Richelieu began to look positively engaging to the French nobles and merchants, and they demanded the dismissal of the Italian cleric. The Queen Mother stubbornly refused—she needed Mazarin. The result of her insistence on retaining the Cardinal was open revolt, a rebellion second in importance only to the Revolution of 1789, and one that cast a similarly baleful light on the stability of the monarchy.

This revolution of 1648–52 was called the Fronde, deriving its name from the slings the Parisian street fighters used to hurl stones. It was eventually suppressed, but the rebels were granted some concessions. More important, though, was its effect on Louis XIV: on reaching his majority, he dismissed both Mazarin and his mother and moved out of town. He was, quite reasonably, suspicious of Paris; this was why he built Versailles, some miles from the city. He made it large enough to entertain simultaneously a substantial proportion of the nobility, for he was, with equal cause, suspicious of the nobles too, and he thought it wise to keep them under as constant surveillance as he could manage.

Louvre and Tuilerie Gardens

As a result of the Sun King's desire to avoid treachery among his subjects, the court life at Versailles was brilliant during his lifetime and that of his great-grandson, Louis XV. From every part of France the nobles flocked to enjoy the fantastic entertainments provided for them by the king. They rented or built town houses, they spent fortunes to live on the scale that the life of Versailles demanded—and, in the process, many were ruined financially. Worse, by remaining under the king's eyes, they had to neglect the domains from which their wealth derived. This was fatal for them—and for Louis XVI; while the nobles were playing at Versailles, the peasants back home were rallying to the cause of revolution.

Pre-Revolutionary Paris was a vivid, gay city, decadent, brilliant, with hospitality for every new idea that came along—not only because the aristocratic citizens who presided over the salons were bored with their leisure, but because they truly welcomed innovation. Voltaire could openly criticize the life at court with comparative impunity. Jean-Jacques Rousseau, who was not sponsored by the nobility, found himself more constrained—but then his ideas were far more advanced than Voltaire's. He told Paris that there was a moral contract between king and country. The implication was plain: the king, so involved with keeping his eye on the nobles, had lost sight of the rest of France. Paris listened to Rousseau; more important perhaps was the fact that the Parisians were given no chance to lose sight of the king. His emissaries were everywhere, collecting taxes that seemed to increase each year to pay for the extravagant wars and the extravagant mistresses of Louis XV. Taxes alone may not have been so bad, but the ungainly and inefficient French economy, frail in the best of times, was on the point of collapse. Paris was hungry.

Marie Antoinette, a good, though rather silly, woman, was the queen of Louis XVI, the fifth Bourbon king who came to the throne in 1774. Louis had no pretensions to wisdom; indeed, it is ironic that his main virtue was virtue itself. Unique among French kings, he appears to have been a man of moderate habits. But it was he who paid with his life for the profligacy of his ancestors, and it was his wife who helped to put his neck beneath the blade of the guillotine. When told that the people of Paris were demanding bread, she probably did not say, "Let them eat cake." The point is that she might very well have said it; she had said and done equally foolish things. The report of this remark was no help to the crumbling monarchy. Marie Antoinette was executed soon after her husband, for the same crime— being of royal blood in a very poor season for royalty.

Some time before the guillotine ended the lives of Louis XVI and Marie Antoinette, a mob, on the fourteenth of July, 1789, had attacked the Bastille, where a number of citizens were being held on royal *lettres de cachet*. These were warrants issued by the crown, on which political enemies could be held indefinitely without any formal charge. Within days, all of France was in arms. A provisional government was established by men whose names adorn the streets of Paris and of many other cities and towns across the land—Danton, Robespierre, Marat, and, most remarkable of all, Talleyrand, who had an incredible instinct for knowing when to jump from a doomed bandwagon. Despite some minor skirmishes, and despite the efforts of foreign nations to come to the aid of the deposed monarchy, the Revolution, for its first few years was quite orderly. Some streets were barricaded—but then, the French always have liked to barricade their streets. It was only when the Revolutionaries quarreled among themselves that the Revolution became the Terror, and no one was safe from the guillotine. For more than a year, the rolling wheels of the tumbrels echoed through the streets of Paris day and night. When the Terror ended on July 27, 1794, some 4000 people had been "legally" murdered. The long Revolution itself had claimed tens of thousands of lives. Not until the Russian Revolution of 1917 would there be anything so bloody.

By the time Napoleon Bonaparte, a general who had been victorious against the foreign armies that were attempting to intervene, seized power in a *coup d'état,* in 1799; whatever the Revolution had accomplished had been washed away in blood. Only the peasant had profited; he had legal possession of the land he had been tilling for the nobility. The Catholic Church had been relieved of most of its land and treasure, as well as its responsibility for education. In the absence of royal authority, there was no authority at all.

Jeanne d'Arc in the Place des Pyramides

Bonaparte, hero of France and scourge of Europe, built a number of monuments to himself in Paris. Among the best known are the two arches of triumph, the one at the Etoile and the other in the Tuileries, and the Vendôme Column. To Bonaparte, too, Paris owes the arcades of the Rue de Rivoli, with its fashionable shops. He was also the author of a tradition which, in succeeding years, has given the nation a great deal of trouble and not a little embarrassment: the force of the army in politics. Only in Germany has the military taken so strong a part in public affairs.

Because the great military academy, St. Cyr, was in Paris, the focus of army life has—like almost everything else—centered here. Following the departure of Napoleon to his ultimate reward at St. Helena, there were at least three attempts by army factions to seize power in France, and several affairs involving the military in some rather unseemly ways. It was, the visitor will recall, the French army that forced the return of General de Gaulle to politics in 1958—its role then, at best, only quasi-legal.

The years from 1815 to 1870 brought what is often described as "ferment" to Paris. Not only governments, but forms of governments came and went with dazzling haste. The Bourbons returned for a time as constitutional kings, acknowledging that the populace had, after all, some rights and liberties. Louis Philippe, a timid fellow, was the last of this great family to serve France as ruler. When history caught up with him in 1848—that year of revolution all over Europe —Louis Philippe was prepared. He had a taxi waiting outside the palace, in which he departed with his family, abdicating the throne. Following three abortive years of acrimonious debate—called the Second Republic—the age of the Second Empire opened. This was presided over by Napoleon III, nephew of the great Bonaparte. But Napoleon III's only resemblance to his audacious forebear existed in his imagination. It is true that under his rule French colonial holdings were greatly increased, but it also is true that he permitted himself to be lured into a catastrophic war with Prussia that resulted in the downfall of his regime and the loss to France of both Alsace and Lorraine. The best thing he did was to employ the brilliant Baron Haussmann to design the Bois de Boulogne and to build the magnificent boulevards and avenues of modern Paris.

Modern Paris—the Palais de Chaillot

The Prussians besieged Paris and controlled most of northern France. After surrender terms were arranged in 1871, the Parisians once more had to decide what sort of government they should try. The Third Republic was the result, an arrangement that seemed perfectly in harmony with the French personality, since it reflected the reluctance of the people to be governed at all.

Following the unfortunate events of 1870–71, Paris—which, since the later days of the Capets, had been the West's great center of education and good manners, the scene of free discussion of all topics, the birthplace of French literature—became as well the birthplace of a great and truly French art. Since the Renaissance, French painting and sculpture had been largely derivative, influenced by the Italians, the Germans, the Dutch, and the Flemish. The explanation for this may lie in the fact that Paris was so receptive to ideas from every land that there was little room for native creative thought to flourish. It may be that the Revolution and its unhappy aftermath of confusion and defeat released forces that previously had been submerged. Or it may simply have been that when Daguerre perfected the photographic process, French painters no longer felt the need to produce pictures which were literal translations of nature and fantasy.

Impressionism is Paris' gift to art; it brought an absolute revolution in painting, a new renaissance. The great impressionist painters —Monet, Sisley, Renoir, Pissarro, and their successors, Seurat, Gauguin, Toulouse-Lautrec—all were French. Within a generation, the process of centuries had been reversed: Paris was now influencing the world of art. Soon impressionism was reflected in music, which had also been derivative. Debussy, Fauré, Ravel, all were influenced by this new concept. Of earlier French composers, perhaps only Hector Berlioz can be said to have been original—and recognition of his qualities was long in coming.

It is the Paris of from 1870 to 1914 that we think of even today as the City of Light. During this time, France was everything we regard as French—gay, prosperous, influential in foreign, as well as intellectual and business matters. And that Paris is the city we recognize today, despite some significant architectural encroachments which have altered its skyline in recent years. The "fin de siècle" was one of glory and decadence for France, and nowhere was it better demonstrated than in Paris. Shadows of this glory are easy to find in the graciousness the city still possesses. The decadence is more difficult to recall. The Boulanger Affair is an example—an attempt to stage a coup d'état in which an amiable general was persuaded that he would be another Bonaparte; fortunately for France, Boulanger did not have the courage of his supporters' convictions. The Dreyfus Case is another instance—the disgraceful performance of

an army whose leaders were violently anti-Semitic seeking to blame
the innocent Captain Dreyfus for espionage of which an Alsatian
nobleman was guilty.

Issues such as these rocked and divided Paris. The capital awaited
the outbreak of World War I to produce unity. But the war also pro-
duced disaster. The French lost more soldiers from 1914 to 1918 than
any other nation except far more populous Russia, and the war was
fought, in the west, almost entirely on French soil. Despite the return
to France of the provinces of Alsace and Lorraine, the nation was—
in the postwar period—badly demoralized. The frightful loss of men
proved catastrophic. France's leadership had to be entrusted to the
hands of men who were a generation too old for the task, and there
were few qualified younger men to replace them. Unwilling and unable to cope with the rise of Hitler, the governments of France rose
and fell like the vast tides in the Bay of Mont St. Michel. There were
steadily worsening economic problems. The population was becoming increasingly captious and fractious. Corruption and even treason
were evidenced constantly. In 1934, another abortive coup d'état was
attempted. Members of the *Croix de Feu,* a Hitler-oriented mob,
marched through the streets of Paris. With war a certainty, indus-
trialists refused to permit their factories to operate more than eight
hours a day; they said that it would wear out their machinery. There
were demands that the government be decentralized, that authority
revert to the provinces of pre-Revolutionary times. The army, until
far too late, believed that the coming war would be fought as World
War I had been waged—in trenches. It placed its reliance on the
Maginot Line, a fantastic series of underground fortifications, which
guarded the French frontier with Germany. Yet when war came, the
Nazis roared through Belgium; the Maginot Line stopped not a single German division.

The role that Paris played in the fall of France cannot be calculated; it was here that the true demoralization had taken place, here
that cabinets played idiot's delight while the house in which they
played was in flames. It was here, too, following the defeat, that incredible acts of individual courage took place. The puppet French
government, under the aged Marshal Pétain, had been installed at
Vichy; Paris was the center of German occupation, an uneasy occupation at best. Guerilla activities constantly harassed the enemy;
and when, in the summer of 1944, it became known that liberation
was momentarily at hand, the citizens of Paris staged a three-day
insurrection that threatened to cut off the German retreat from the
city. Once again, the streets were barricaded, gunfire was heard at
every corner.

Between the moment of liberation and the creation, in 1946, of
the Fourth Republic—virtually a carbon copy of the Third—was

the first era of General de Gaulle. With his admirable understanding of French history, de Gaulle refused to have any part of the
Fourth Republic; it would, he felt, produce a repetition of the
foibles and catastrophes of the Third. And to a degree, this was
true. The average life of a government under the new constitution
was eight months. France was embroiled in a struggle in Indochina
that drained her treasury of hard currencies, and later in similar
difficulties in Algeria. The economy, though, flourished as never before, but it was accompanied by an inflation that all but vitiated the
vast industrial growth.

Paris, in the postwar period, changed very little. The city was the
scene of continuous intellectual ferment, of endless discussions in
salons and cafés, and in the Chamber of Deputies; it was constantly
disturbed by violent street demonstrations and general strikes, many
Communist-inspired.

In the summer of 1958, the army forced the hand of the government. "Give us de Gaulle," they said in effect, "or there will be civil
war." The general, however, was not so eager to assume control. He
wanted no part of a coup d'état. If the French really wanted him,
they could have him only on his own terms—a brand new constitution, a Fifth Republic. He got what he demanded, by a majority
that would have been gratifying in a police state, and which was
overwhelming in a nation not known for its unanimity of opinion
about anything.

Armed with a constitution providing for stability of leadership, de
Gaulle steered a severely nationalistic course until 1968 when
pent-up resentment over many of his measures led to major
disruptions and strikes, culminating in his retirement. Modified
Gaullist politics nevertheless continued to dominate the French
scene until the 1974 election of a young liberal president, Valéry
Giscard d'Estaing, who is now faced with reconciling the fundamen-
tal French need for stability with their overt passion for change. In
contrast to the loftiness of his predecessors, Giscard has attempted
to humanize his office by bringing himself closer to the people; but
are superficial measures going to satisfy the French and ease the
anxiety they feel about their own and their country's place in today's
world?

Only time will provide the answer. Of this, however, we may be
sure: when the answer comes, Paris will give it.

CHAPTER *3*

THINGS TO KNOW ABOUT PARIS

At the risk of being repetitive, let us say that Paris is a city that will fulfill all your needs—and that goes as much for the practical everyday things of life as it does for the needs of the spirit. This chapter is the one you read when you want to know where to buy shaving cream (your favorite American brand) or to know the number to call if you have a toothache. It also will tell you how much to tip the washroom attendant and how to use a French telephone. This is a chapter of *practical* information—facts that you will want to know before you go and after you get there.

PLANNING

Climate. The weather in Paris is somewhat like that of New York City except that it is more temperate; cooler in summer and warmer in winter. Spring and fall are generally balmy, ideal for walking and sight-seeing. There are many bright, sunny days in winter too, and it rarely goes below freezing. Most hotels and public buildings are not heated as much as they are in the United States, and so Parisians wear heavier dresses or suits indoors, and lighter coats outdoors. Be prepared for rainy days (soft, misty rains, rather than driving ones) in the fall and winter.

What to Bring. Experienced globe-trotters have learned the joy of traveling as light as possible. You would be wise not to take more clothes than can be packed into one large suitcase. You will need the same kind of clothes in Paris as in any other large metropolitan city. For women, suits, slacks, or dresses and sturdy walking shoes are

Children at play in Montmartre

right in the daytime (except for hot summer days), and dressier clothes and high-heeled slippers in the evening. Shorts, and extreme sports clothes are out of place in Paris, save them for resort wear. French men dress conservatively in the streets, even in summer, and a short-sleeved sports shirt marks you as a tourist. Parisians have grown accustomed to seeing Americans comfortably attired that way for sight-seeing in hot weather, but any man will look—and feel—conspicuous in a good restaurant without a jacket and tie. Formal evening clothes are not necessary except in the winter if you expect to attend gala performances at the Opéra or Friday dancing *soirées* at a supper club like Maxim's.

Cleaning and Laundry. Most large hotels offer a two-day laundry service, and dry cleaning can be done in a day; this service is much less expensive, however, if you deal directly with a commercial dry-cleaner. But you will feel freer to move about if you are not dependent on laundries. Modern materials like dacron drip-dry shirts, nylon underwear, and wash-and-wear dresses are the perfect solution. If you choose your clothes wisely, you will also eliminate the need for taking along an electric iron. There is such wide variation in electric voltage and outlet types in France that your iron usually won't work in hotels, even though it has been sold as adapted for European current. Any hotel will do simple pressing quickly.

Exchanging Money. Most Americans carry their money in the form of travelers' checks. They are safer than cash, and easily converted. The following places have exchange booths which stay open after regular banking hours: the *Invalides* air terminal, open every day, including Sat., Sun., and holidays, from 7 A.M. to 11:30 P.M.; the *Porte Maillot* air terminal open seven days a week from 9 A.M. to 7 P.M.; the *Gare de Lyon*, open from 6:30 A.M. to 11:00 P.M.; *Orly, Le Bourget* and *Roissy* airports, open 24 hours a day. Exchange booths are open all day including weekends at the following railroad stations: *Gare de l'Est, Gare St. Lazare, Gare d'Austerlitz.*

The present official rate of exchange is 4.24 francs to the dollar—which means one franc is worth about 24¢. However, the exact rate you get will vary depending on where you make the exchange. A French or American bank or American Express on Rue Scribe will give you the best rate (somewhat under the official rate). If you want to change money at a hotel, restaurant or shop, you will probably pay for the convenience with a small (and varying) discount.

TRANSPORTATION

If you have the time and really want to know Paris, you'll explore mostly by foot, of course. Buy the pocket-sized *Plan Taride* which lists every street, *arrondissement,* Métro station, and bus line. It has pages of really good detail maps. The public transportation system

The boat pond in the Tuileries

of Paris is a marvel of logic and clarity, just made for tourists.

Taxis. Taxis are easily found everywhere in Paris, except during rush hours and at lunch and dinner time. However, a phone call to 205 77–77, 735 22–22, 267 28–30, or 587 67–89 will summon a radio-taxi at any hour—the fare starts from the point where the driver received the call. Regular taxi rates are quite reasonable by American standards, the daytime tariff starting at 3^{50} francs and going up 80 centimes for each kilometer. The night rate (from 10:00 P.M. to 6:30 A.M.) is double. Baggage and other additional charges are posted in the cab. You can recognize an empty cab by an upright meter flag with the word *libre* on it. The flag is covered when the driver doesn't want passengers. In front of night clubs or de luxe hotels, you may encounter taxis without meters. Be sure to agree on the price before you hire one; otherwise it will be two or three times the regular rate. Better still, walk down the street and take a metered cab. Don't believe the myth that Paris drivers speak English. Hardly any do. If you don't trust your French, just write out where you want to go. Standard tip is 10 to 15 per cent.

Métro. Traffic in the city is so heavy nowadays that the subway is the quickest, as well as the cheapest, way of getting around. The Paris Métro is marvelously efficient and easy to understand. Each station has a huge map at the entrance, with a circle showing where you are and what line to take to get to your destination. Principal stations also have electric maps that light up when you push the button next to the stop you want and indicate the exact route, including any changes, that will get you there. Everything is so clearly marked on maps and signs that a few rides will easily make you a Métro expert. A booklet (*carnet*) for ten rides is more convenient and economical than buying individual tickets. There is one first-class car, of a different color, in the center of each train; its only advantage is during rush hours when it is less crowded than second-class cars. Trains run from 5:30 in the morning to 12:50 at night (last departure).

Buses. Traveling by bus is slower, but much pleasanter, because it allows you to see the face of Paris. Over fifty bus lines crisscross the city. They are designated by numbers, and the route and destination are clearly marked on the side, front, and rear of each bus. You can use your *carnet* of subway tickets on buses as well; otherwise you can buy your tickets individually, at a slightly higher price, from the bus conductor. Longer rides require more than one ticket. All Parisian buses now have an automatic ticket-punching mechanism located near the driver's seat. Be sure to hold on to your ticket until you get off. Buses stop only on signal, so don't forget to ring the bell when you come to your stop, and to flag the bus when you want to get on. Parisians are amazingly orderly (for Parisians) about getting on buses. They actually stand in line on the sidewalk. The first buses of the day leave their starting points at 5:30 A.M., and most stop running at 9:30 P.M., although some do run until 12:30. Thereafter, they run every hour from the Châtelet (1:30–5:30 A.M.) and from the various *portes* on the city limits (1–5 A.M.).

Carriages. For the most pleasant, if expensive, way of traveling, there are still a few old-fashioned horse-drawn *fiacres*, found mainly around the Opéra, the Eiffel Tower, the Tuileries, and the Champs-Elysées. Carriages have no meters, so be sure to make a price with the driver beforehand.

Railroads. Paris has six railway stations, each going to a different part of the country. Trains are frequent and excellent, holding the record for the world's fastest runs.

Gare de l'Est, for points east: Alsace-Lorraine, Germany, the Basle area of Switzerland, and central Europe;

Gare du Nord, for northern France: Boulogne, Dunkirk, Calais channel crossings, Belgium, and Holland;

Gare de Lyon, for Lyon and points south: the Mediterranean, Italy, Austria, Geneva and Lausanne in Switzerland, and Yugoslavia;

Gare d' Austerlitz (or Gare d'Orléans), for southwest region: the Loire, Auvergne, Midi, Spain, and Portugal;

Gare Montparnasse, for the west: Brittany and Anjou;

Gare St. Lazare, another for points west: Normandy, and for boat trains to Cherbourg and Le Havre.

For all general information about French and international trains call 522 94-00 (English-speaking operators).

Air travel. Paris has three air fields: *Le Bourget,* ten miles to the northeast; *Orly,* eleven miles south; and the ultra modern *Charles de Gaulle* airport at Roissy, thirteen miles to the north. The *Aérogare des Invalides* is the town terminal for air service to Orly, and the *Aérogare de la Porte Maillot* services the other two airports. For twenty-four-hour information service about arrival and departure of planes telephone Orly, 707 85–55, Le Bourget, 833 05–90, and Roissy, 862 12–12.

Car Rentals. Small cars are best for narrow country roads (and city traffic) and will save you money on gas which costs three times what you pay in the U.S. Prices per day run $8.00 to $18.00 (including insurance, oil, lubrication), plus gas and 6¢ to 15¢ per km. ($\frac{3}{5}$ of a mile). From November to March rates are 10% lower. A deposit of $70 is required. They will ask to see your American license.

The major companies: *Avis:* Orly Airport (587 51–41), Le Bourget Airport (208 98–90), 60 Rue de Ponthieu (359 0383), 99 Ave. General de Gaulle in Neuilly (722 13–74). *Hertz:* Orly (687 10–44), Le Bourget (284 38–01), Aérogare des Invalides (551 20–37), Rue Saint-Ferdinand (754 99–69), to reserve a Hertz car in any city of Europe (788 73–00). *Mattei:* 207 Rue de Bercy near Gare de Lyon (345 56–10). *Europcars,* 42 Ave. de Saxe (645 21–09). You can also rent at American Express or any other large travel agency.

There are also limousines for hire with excellent chauffeurs who double as guides. These cost more, of course—about ninety to one hundred fifty dollars a day, depending on the type of car—but the prices seem less prohibitive when divided among four or more persons. Your hotel concierge can arrange to hire one for you.

Sight-seeing. If your stay in Paris is brief, or if you want a quick picture of the city, an organized tour is the best way of seeing the major sights. Check with your hotel concierge or any large travel agency which specializes in air-conditioned bus tours led by English-speaking guides: try *American Express,* 11 Rue Scribe (742 75–00); *Cityrama* at 2 Rue du 29 Juillet (260 76–87); or *Thomas Cook & Sons,* 2 Place de la Madeleine (260 33–20). They also have tours to nearby Chateau of the Loire, Chartres, Versailles, etc. *Rapid Pullman,* 3 Places des Pyramides (260 31–01), has bus tours.

Tourist Information. Besides these agencies, there are several French national organizations (with English-speaking staffs) equipped to give general information and pamphlets about Paris and all the provinces of France.

Secrétariat d'État au Tourisme, 8 Ave. de l'Opéra (742 11–39);
Bureau National de Tourisme, 127 Ave. des Champs-Elysées (720 12–80);
Touring-Club de France, 65 Ave. de la Grande-Armée (727 89–89);
Automobile-Club de France, 6 Place de la Concorde (265 34–70).

Paris Welcome Information Offices. The main office, Accueil de France, 127 Champs-Elysées (720 90–16), has Telex communication with other parts of France, and can make reservations for you in Cannes, Tours, etc. The other offices in Paris can be found at the Air Terminal des Invalides (705 82–81), Air Terminal de la Porte Maillot (758 22–45), Gare du Nord (526 94–82), Gare St. Lazare (522 74–01), Gare de Lyon (343 33–24), and Gare de l'Est (607 17–73). These offices are staffed by Paris Hostesses who have all information, probable and improbable, at their multilingual fingertips.

River Boats. The *Bateaux-Mouches* are modern excursion boats, equipped with orchestras, restaurants, and snack bars. The boats cruise up the banks of the Seine as far as the Bois de Boulogne on trips that last for 1, 1½, or 2½ hours. The evening trip, with dinner on board, is particularly delightful when the monuments on shore are illuminated. Boats leave from a wharf near the Place de l'Alma. For details, call 225 96–10.

Vedettes Paris-Tour Eiffel is a new service, running smaller comfortable launches from the Pont d'Iéna every twenty minutes. English-speaking guides are available. Their special daytime tour, which includes a river drive, a visit to wine cellars (*caves*) with wine-tasting, and lunch in the Eiffel Tower must be booked through a travel agent. Call 551 33–08 for information.

THE PARIS SCHEDULE

In general, Paris stores and businesses stay open later than their American counterparts, but some of them close for a two-hour stretch at lunch time, and stores (except food shops) are closed on Mondays, too. During the months of July and August, Parisians leave for their holidays, and a great many shops and restaurants display their *Clôture Annuelle* signs. Don't start out for any restaurant in summer before checking.

Banks are open weekdays 9 A.M. to 4 P.M. They close on Saturdays and at noon on the day *before* a legal holiday. Large banks keep one wicket open on Saturdays in the summer for foreign money exchange.

Department stores are open from 9:15 A.M. to 6:30 P.M., except Sundays and holidays. Twice a week, usually on Wednesdays and Fridays, some of them remain open until 9:30 P.M.

Travel agencies, transportation offices, the American Consulate, and the United States Embassy are closed on Saturday, though the latter always leaves one staff member on duty for emergencies.

All banks, offices, museums, and sight-seeing places are closed on the following public holidays: Jan. 1, Easter Monday, May 1

Paris at night: fireworks over Sacré Coeur—and Pigalle

(the French Labor Day, when the streets are filled with lily of the valley, but not a single taxi), Ascension Day and Whit Monday in May, July 14 (Bastille Day), Aug. 15 (Assumption Day), Nov. 1 (All Saints' Day), November 11 (Armistice Day), and on Christmas Day. Holidays falling on a Sunday are followed by Monday closings.

TIPPING

Although tipping has been mentioned in various other chapters, this will summarize it in one place. Americans have a reputation for over-tipping. It gains them no respect and makes things much harder for the people who come after them.

Hotels. The service charge is almost always included on the bill. It does not, however, cover the baggage porter, who should get one franc or more, according to the number of bags, and the concierge, whose tip will depend on how many things he does for you. The telephone operator, if she does some translating for you, and the chambermaid, if she does any pressing, mending, or other special service, should be given small additional tips.

Restaurants. Even if service is included (*compris*), many people leave a small extra tip (at least one franc) for the waiter. If service is *non-compris*, 12 to 15 per cent is expected, or as high as 20 per cent, in a de luxe restaurant. The wine steward (*sommelier*) should be tipped separately, not less than one franc, and more if the service is especially good or if you are dining in a de luxe restaurant.

Cloakrooms. One to two francs, depending on the place.

Washrooms. Fifty centimes to one franc.

Theaters and Movies. Ushers definitely expect to be tipped: In an elegant Champs-Elysées theater one to two francs for each ticket; in a neighborhood movie at least one franc. Have your money ready before you step into the darkened house so you won't have to fumble for it and perhaps give too much.

Taxis. 10 to 15 per cent.

ENTERTAINMENT

The most Parisian of all Paris spectacles is Bastille Day, the 14th of July. On that day the entire city bursts alive, bands play, and the streets, filled with crowds, are hung with colored streamers. Brilliant fireworks explode in the sky, and the city celebrates until the small hours of the morning. (The best vantage points for viewing the fireworks are the Pont Neuf and the Pont de Grenelle.)

This happens but once a year, but the famed night life of Paris—the cabarets, and boîtes, the music halls—continues night after night, and there is more of it than in any other city. For those whose stay in Paris is short, or for women without escorts, the most sensible and economical thing is to take one of the travel agencies' guided tours. These one-night excursions generally include three different types of clubs, such as the Moulin Rouge dance hall in Montmartre, a small typically French singing cabaret, and end with champagne at one of the more elegant night clubs like the Lido.

To find out what is playing at the theaters, movies, ballets, etc. consult the excellent weekly guide *Pariscope* and/or the *Officiel des Spectacles*.

NIGHT CLUBS

Paris night clubs run the gamut from sedate supper clubs to the most boisterous cabarets. In both, you may dance between the shows, and both are quite expensive. Champagne is usually the obligatory drink; the minimum charge per person for half a bottle is about 60 francs. If you prefer Scotch or other hard liquor, a round of these will come to as much as a bottle of champagne. Some close one summer month. It's always wise to phone for reservations in advance.

OPERA, MADELEINE, CHAMPS-ELYSEES DISTRICT

Crazy Horse Saloon, 12 Ave. George V (225 69–69). An old favorite—renowned temple honoring the eternal feminine . . . stripper. Champagne not obligatory.

Lido, 78 Ave. des Champs Elysées (359 11–61). An all time favorite for everyone.

La Belle Epoque, 38 Rue des Petits Champs (073 69–18). Dining, floor show, and/or dancing.

Les Sons Gêne, 12 Rue de Marignan (359 58–64). The show is excellent and most people you see here are famous in their own way.

Diner Spectacle de la Tour Eiffel, (551 19–51). A beautiful show on the first floor of the famous tower and a fine dinner; open every day. Expensive.

Villa d'Este, 4 Rue Ars. Houssaye (359 78–44). Smart dining, dancing, supping. Amusing show, if you know some French.

MONTMARTRE DISTRICT

Bal du Moulin Rouge, Place Blanche (606 00–19). Dance hall, immortalized by Renoir and Toulouse-Lautrec, features the traditional can-can and first-rate show. Closed Jan. and Feb.

Monseigneur, 94 Rue d'Amsterdam (874 25–35). Beautiful romantic setting; serenading violinists. Dress on Fridays. Closed Sun.

Shéhérazade, 3 Rue de Liège (874 85–20). An Arabian Nights sort of place, lushly elegant. Russian music and cuisine. Very expensive.

MONTPARNASSE, ST. GERMAIN-DES-PRES DISTRICT

L'Alcazar, 62 Rue Mazarine (633 64–94). Another boite à la mode for another enjoyable evening. Closed Sundays.

Barbary Coast Saloon, 11 Rue Jules Chaplain (033 68–87). Discothèque from 9 P.M. to dawn.

La Grande Séverine, 7 Rue St. Séverin (325 50–04). Chic Russian atmosphere, and music till dawn at their discothèque. Expensive. Closed Mondays.

CHANSONNIERS

The typically French entertainment of the *chansonnier* features an intimate atmosphere, the singing of old songs and ballads, sometimes poetry recitals, clever sketches, pantomimes or satiric comments and friendly insults—all in good fun. The true Chansonnier hardly exists anymore, but the following places offer something of the old flavor, with the emphasis more on folk-singing than on skits. The physical setting of some of these clubs are at least quite different from the usual night club. The *Caveau des Oubliettes,* for example, is located in the catacombs of the church of St. Julien-le-Pauvre. You will appreciate the music, the clever pantomime and the intrinsically different atmosphere, but you need an understanding of French to catch the subtleties of this kind of entertainment.

MONTMARTRE DISTRICT

Chez Ma Cousine, Place du Tertre (227 78–29). Good dinner and a show in the old Montmartre fashion (best to know French).

Le Lapin Agile, 22 Rue des Saules (606 85–87). Famous old haunt of Montmartre artists and writers. Much atmosphere, dim lights, paintings on walls, old French ballads. Closed Mon.

LEFT BANK

L'Abbaye, 6 bis Rue Guillaume Apollinaire (033 27–77). Near St. Germain-des-Prés. Guitar-playing and folk-songs, in French and English. A young American hangout. Closed Sundays.

La Galerie 55, 55 Rue de Seine (326 63–51). Music, song and laughter in the heart of the art gallery district.

Caveau des Oubliettes, 11 Rue St. Julien (033 94–97). Old French songs in a historic 13th-century crypt.

Le Petrin, 86 Rue Mouffetard. Intimate rendezvous for those who enjoy old songs and poetry. Inexpensive.

MAINLY JAZZ

For dancing: **Whiskey A Go-Go,** 57 Rue de Seine (633 74–99). **Le Caméléon,** 57 Rue St. André des Arts (326 64–40). **Mambo Club,** 20 Rue Cujas (033 89–21). **Le Tabou,** 33 Rue Dauphine (633 33–95).
For Le Jazz (Left Bank): **Caveau de la Huchette,** 5 Rue de la Huchette (326 65–05), featuring Dixieland. **Trois Mailletz,** 56 Rue Galande (033 00–79).
For Le Jazz (Right Bank): **Newport,** 18 Rue des Quatre Vents (325 56–10). **Club Pierre Charron,** 52 Rue Pierre Charron (359 35–30). **Slow Club,** 130 Rue de Rivoli (233 84–30). **Le Calvados,** 40 Rue Pierre Ier de Serbie (359 27–28). Open 24 hours a day, seven days a week. Piano music from 11 P.M. on. **Harry's Bar,** 5 Rue Daunou (073 73–00). The original American bar in Paris. Cocktail lounge downstairs with music from 10 P.M. to 2 A.M.

MUSIC HALLS

Paris music halls sometimes offer a mixture of vaudeville, top pop singers, and burlesque—but all in a tame theater atmosphere. These shows are very popular and crowded, so make reservations well in advance. Prices range from 20 to 80 francs.

Bobino, 20 Rue de la Gaité (033 30–49). Famous Montparnasse vaudeville theater.
Casino de Paris, 16 Rue de Clichy (874 26–22). Now the home ground of Roland Petit and Zizi Jeanmaire.
Folies Bergère, 32 Rue Richer (770 98–49). Beautiful nudes and marvelous spectacles.
Mayol, 10 Rue de L'Echiquier (770 95–08). French and non-French burlesque.
Olympia, 28 Boulevard des Capucines (742 25–49). Top vaudeville headliners.

Your choice: Guignol puppets in the Bois de Boulogne and the Follies Bergère

The grand staircase at the Opéra

OPERA

The main opera season begins in September and extends through June; the ballet takes over in July. There are two opera houses. The *Opéra* is the elegant and famous structure at the Place de l'Opéra (073 95–26), which now features a new ceiling by the painter Chagall. Friday night is gala night here when most Parisians dress formally. It shuts down completely in August. The second opera house is the *Opéra Studio de Paris* located at 5 Rue Favart (742 72–00) which presents lighter opera; it is closed Wednesdays and Thursdays. Tickets, which go on sale a week before a performance, vary from about 10 to 40 francs.

BALLET

Parisians are very fond of ballet and performances are given three or four times weekly during June and July, as well as six times monthly during the opera season. The Théâtre National de l'Opéra is an excellent repertory company that presents works in the classical tradition. Other popular ballet companies like those of *Roland Petit* also give performances throughout the year in Paris. Prices range from about 10 to 50 francs.

THEATERS

The theater is a most active force in Parisian life, and a wide variety of plays is offered in more than sixty theaters. It is easier to obtain theater tickets on short notice in Paris than in New York, because seats are not sold for more than two weeks in advance.

The *Comédie Française*, the great national repertory company, presents the classical works of France's greatest playwrights, such as Molière and Corneille, which you can enjoy whether or not you know French. It also stages more recent comedies. While its permanent home at the Place du Théâtre Français is being renovated, the company will appear at the *Théâtre de Marigny* (742 27–31), so check the local press before setting out for tickets. The famous Madeleine Renaud–Jean Louis Barrault company (named for the fine actor and actress who direct and act in many of its productions) is located at the *Théâtre d'Orsay*, 7 Quai Anatole France (548 65–90).

Paris is the kind of theater town where an Ionesco double bill plays to packed audiences for a decade, where *Hair* is a super hit, and *Jesus Christ Superstar* is a superb failure.

Shows start at 8:30 P.M. and some houses also have an early show 6:30 P.M. A good seat will cost you about 25 francs. If you buy through a ticket bureau expect to pay 20% more.

Tipping: It is customary to tip the usherette who shows you to your seat. If you have an expensive seat, a tip of one franc is right, while 50 centimes will do for an inexpensive seat. *Programs* are skimpy and expensive (and optional)—three francs or more.

CONCERTS

The concert season for orchestras such as the Pasdeloup, Radio, Conservatoire, Colonne and Lamoureux is from October through March or April. However, individual concerts are given all year long in the two major concert halls, the Salle Pleyel and the Salle Gaveau and in the Théâtre de Chaillot. The Conservatory Orchestra also gives concerts every Sunday, all winter, at the Théâtre des Champs Elysées. *Pariscope* will tell you what individual artists are performing while you are in town.

CHILDREN'S THEATERS

If you are traveling with children, going to one of the children's theaters is a most pleasant experience. There is a marionette show every Wednesday, Saturday and Sunday afternoon at the *Théâtre de Marionettes de Luxembourg* in the Luxembourg Gardens. This is beautifully done and highly entertaining, even if you don't understand French. Another marionette company performs on the same afternoons in the Jardin d'Acclimatation in the Bois de Boulogne.

MOTION PICTURES

American and British films are very popular in Paris. Make sure you check the movie listing (in the weekly guides or in newspapers) for V. O. (Version Originale) which means the films are shown in their original language, usually with French subtitles. It is important to find out just when a show begins because movies are not always continuous and you may even have trouble being seated once the feature film has started. Remember that the usher who shows you to your seat should be tipped, at least 50 centimes per person.

GENERAL INFORMATION

Medical Care. The American Hospital in Paris is an excellent hospital with a predominantly American staff. The hospital will supply names over the telephone (637 72-00) of American doctors and dentists in Paris. For medical emergencies in the middle of the night or on Sundays, the nearest Commissariat of Police will supply you with the name of a nearby doctor.

Pharmacies. Except for the modish new "Drugstores" at the top of the Champs-Elysées, on the Ave. Matignon and on the Blvd. St. Germain, Paris pharmacies carry only drugs and toilet articles. They are open from 9:00 A.M. to 8:00 P.M., except on Sundays and Monday morning. However, one pharmacy in each district stays open at those times; the door of the nearest pharmacy displays its name and location. There are several all-night pharmacies, notably on the Place Pigalle and at Montparnasse.

The following drugstores stock American brands (usually two or three times as expensive as in the U.S.) and have English-speaking clerks:

British and American Pharmacy, 1 Rue Auber.
Pharmacie Caron, 24 Rue de la Paix.
Pharmacie des Champs-Elysées, 62 Ave. des Champs-Eylsées.
Le Drugstore, 133 Ave. des Champs-Elysées.

Beauty Parlors. All of the larger hotels have excellent hairdressing salons (where English is spoken). Fashionable and expensive:

Carita, 11 Faubourg Saint Honoré (265 79-00).
Jacques Dessange, 37 Ave. F.D. Roosevelt (359 31–31).
Charles of the Ritz, 51 Ave. Montaigne (359 55–39).
Elizabeth Arden, 7 Place Vendôme (261 55–55).
Helena Rubinstein, 52 Fg. St. Honoré (265 65–69).
Alexandre, 120 Fg. St. Honoré (225 89–68).

Salons at the department stores are competent and cheaper; open 9:30 A.M. to 5:45 P.M., except Sundays:

Au Printemps, 64 Blvd. Haussmann (744 67–77).
Galeries Lafayette, 40 Blvd. Haussmann (073 01–54).
Au Bon Marché (left bank) 135 Rue du Bac (222 33–00).

Babysitters. If your hotel can't supply one, call the Paris Students' Job Center (Centre Regional des Oeuvres Universitaires et Scolaires) (326 07–49) for a reliable young person. A medical students group, Opération Biberon (033 25–44) also provides babysitters.

Telephone and Telegraph. Public telephones are found on street corners, in post offices, the Métro, railway stations, cafés, and tobacco shops. To make a call you first buy a *jeton* (token) from the cashier. Drop it in the slot, then pick up the receiver, dial, and when someone answers (*not* before) push the button beneath to establish connection. Certain new public phones function with coins rather than tokens. At post offices there are operators to whom you can give your number (in writing), and they will make the connection for you. Long-distance calls are harder because some are dialed and some are not. In Paris you can reach an English-speaking operator by dialing 10 and then 10 again after a shrill tone is heard. Or simpler, ask the concierge or telephone operator at your hotel to make the call for you.

Telegrams and cables can be sent through any post office, open from 8:00 A.M. to 7:00 P.M. every day except Saturday afternoon and Sunday. The central post office at 52 Rue du Louvre is open all night. To send a cable by telephone, dial 523 42–42, or 233 22–11. Telex services are available at the *Office du Tourisme*, 127 Champs-Elysées, daily from 9 A.M. to 6:15 P.M. and Sunday mornings.

Mail. If they don't use their hotel address, most Americans have mail sent to them in care of American Express or their banks in Paris. Air mail is minutely calculated to increase by fifty centimes for every five grams of weight and mounts up rapidly. That's why it is worth investing in the onion-skin stationery which is used for air mail throughout Europe.

Newspapers and Magazines. There is now only one American newspaper printed in Paris, the *International Herald Tribune*. International editions of *Time*, and *Newsweek* appear about the same time that they do in the U.S., and other American and English periodicals are available about a week later.

Lost and Found. Articles turned into the *Service des Objets Trouvés,* 36 Rue des Morillons (15e), can be claimed not before the afternoon following the day of loss. You must go in person, telephone inquiries are not answered. Open daily 8:30–7:00, closed Sat., Sun., holidays. If lost on bus or Métro, articles are kept for one day at terminus of line. It is customary to leave 10 per cent of value as reward.

Sports. You can enjoy any of the sports in Paris that you do at home. There is a *Fédération Française* for golf, tennis, horseback riding, ice skating, mountain climbing, handball, and every other sport you can think of. Your hotel concierge or travel agency can tell you where to apply to the appropriate *Fédération* for temporary membership in the particular sport club that interests you. There are dozens of indoor swimming pools throughout the city, and, in summer, outdoor ones in the Seine. The *Molitor* and the *Deligny* (filtered water), near the Pont de la Concorde, are the best of the public pools.

Among spectator sports, football (Americans call it *soccer*) and bicycle racing are among the most popular. The Davis Cup and other international matches take place in the *Stade Roland-Garros*. The sporting event that all of France follows with passionate interest is the *tour de France,* a bicycle race across the country in July which has its finale in Paris.

Horse racing is extremely popular and attracts large crowds. There are eight major tracks near Paris, featuring races throughout the year: at Chantilly, Longchamps, Auteuil, Saint-Cloud, Vincennes, Maisons-Lafitte, Enghien, and Tremblay. The Grand Steeplechase at Auteuil and the *Grand Prix* at Longchamps on the last two Sundays

One of the most famous of the St. Germain cafés

in June are the most exciting and fashionable races. For information about major events and daily racing consult the newspapers or the weekly *Pariscope*, which lists all sporting events. Betting is controlled by the government, and bets may be placed either at the track, or at pari-mutuel booths in Paris tobacco shops.

Gambling Casinos. The nearest gambling casino to Paris that allows roulette is at Enghien-les-Bains, about 15 miles away. Gambling, like racing, is strictly controlled by the French government, which insures honest results.

Religious Services. Almost all churches in Paris are Catholic, of course. The following have services in English:

ST. JOSEPH'S CHURCH	50 Avenue Hoche (8e).
Protestant	
AMERICAN CHURCH IN PARIS	65 Quai d'Orsay (7e).
AMERICAN CATHEDRAL IN PARIS	23 Ave. George V (8e) (Episcopal, all denominations welcome).
FIRST CHURCH OF CHRIST SCIENTIST	36 Boul. St. Jacques (14e).
SECOND CHURCH OF CHRIST SCIENTIST	58 Boul. Flandrin (16e).
METHODIST CHAPEL	4 Rue Roquépine (8e).
BAPTIST CHURCH	48 Rue de Lille (7e).
SOCIETY OF FRIENDS	114 Rue de Vaugirard (6e).

Paris is not all sights

Jewish

GREAT SYNAGOGUE	44 Rue de la Victoire (9e).
LIBERAL SYNAGOGUE	24 Rue Copernic (16e).

USEFUL ADDRESSES

American Legion	49 Rue Pierre Charron (225 41–93).
American Express *(main office)*	11 Rue Scribe (742 75–00).
American Hospital	63 Boul. Victor-Hugo, Neuilly (637 72–00).
American Library	10 Rue Camou (551 46–82) (books and periodicals in English).
A.A.A.	8 Place de la Concorde (266 43–00).
Bank of America	28 Pl. Vendôme (742 55–26).
Bureau des Objets Trouvés (Lost and Found)	36 Rue des Morrillons.
Chase Manhattan Bank	41 Rue Cambon (073 44–30).
Chief Prefecture de Police	Place Louis-Lépine (260 33–22).
First National City Bank	60 Champs-Elysées (260 33–60).
Morgan Guaranty Trust Co.	14 Place Vendôme (260 35–60).
Thomas Cook & Son	2 Place de la Madeleine (260 33–20).
United States Embassy	2 Ave. Gabriel (near Place de la Concorde) (265 74–60).
Service des Etrangers (for foreigners)	23 Blvd. Ney (607 53–01).

USEFUL FACTS

Drinking water in Paris is just as pure as any in the U.S.

House numbers begin from the end nearest the Seine in streets running north to south, and from the eastern end in east-west streets.

Sounding automobile horns is now forbidden in Paris, except for real emergencies.

Paris is filled to the brim from April to September. Be sure to make a hotel reservation in advance during that period.

The word *hôtel* before such famous buildings as Hôtel Cluny, Hôtel Soubise, etc., does not mean that it is, or ever was, a hotel in our sense of the word. It simply indicates a large building, either a private or public mansion.

In Paris you enter a building on the ground floor (*rez-de-chaussée* or *RC*) and walk up one flight to the first floor (*premier étage*), two flights to the third *(deuxième)*. The basement is called *sous-sol.*

If you find yourself ascending to the second or third floor in darkness, it's probably because you have forgotten to press the mysterious *minuterie*. This is a button at the bottom of the staircase in most apartment houses and some hotels which you push in order to illuminate the stairs for about three minutes. (Saves electricity.)

Always carry your passport with you. You need it for cashing travelers' checks and for other identification purposes.

In any difficulty speak to the nearest policeman or the *Commissaire de Police* at the local police station. For big trouble contact the American Embassy.

You will probably forget those delightful restaurants, shops, and names of people you've met unless you keep a little notebook always with you to jot down the information on the spot.

If you'd like to take home some of those handsome, colored travel posters, you can find them, reasonably priced, at *Direction Général du Tourisme*, 8 Ave. de l' Opéra.

Notre Dame—favorite subject of sidewalk painters

CHAPTER 4

More than any other city in the world, Paris is crowded with the
visible evidence of its glorious past and its exciting present. Even a
quick tour of the principal sights described in this chapter will take
at least a week. But what if you have only two or three days? Luckily,
few cities display their charms more dramatically and openly. An
hour or two spent viewing the sweep of the superb Champs-Elysées,
the magnificent vistas of the Place de la Concorde, the flood-lit night
beauty of the elegant buildings, and lovely parks contrasting with the
intimacy of the crooked little side streets—such things will give you
an immediate feel of the city.

For the visitor who wants to be sure to see the main sights, the most
convenient and least expensive way is to begin with one of the morning or afternoon guided tours run by American Express and other
travel agencies. Such a tour will give you a quick over-all impression of old and new Paris; then you can go back to explore the places
that interest you most. The following list of high spots will remind
you at a glance of the things you shouldn't miss. (All are described
more fully later in this chapter.) You will notice that the best things
in Paris are free. Even this small sampling should capture for you
some of the enchantment that makes Paris the most beautiful city in
the world.

ON THE RIGHT BANK

Arc de Triomphe. From the top of Napoleon's world-renowned triumphal arch you have a magnificent view of all Paris and especially
of the twelve handsome avenues radiating from Place de Gaulle.

St. Germain-des-Prés, one of Paris' oldest churches.

Champs-Elysées. Extending in a broad sweep from Place de Gaulle to the Concorde is the gayest and most elegant boulevard in the world.

Place de la Concorde. The site of the guillotine during the French Revolution, the open vistas of this square make it an incomparable gem. Don't fail to see it flood-lit at night.

The Tuileries. These magnificent formal gardens, which join the Place de la Concorde to the Louvre, are a refreshing beauty spot in the heart of Paris.

The Louvre. The greatest museum in the world. See suggestions for a high-light tour.

Palais Royal. The gardens and arcaded walks of this former royal palace near the Louvre offer old-world quiet and serenity in a bustling part of town.

Place Vendôme. Architecturally one of the handsomest squares in Paris, it is also one of the fashion centers.

L'Opéra. The largest and most elaborate opera house in the world— a symbol of the lavish luxury of the Second Empire.

The Madeleine. This replica of a Greek temple, built by Napoleon to the glory of the French army, is now a fashionable church.

Palais de Chaillot. An extraordinary example of modern French architecture, it has lovely gardens overlooking the Seine, a beautiful theater, and four interesting museums.

Place du Tertre. The village charm of old Montmartre still exists in this little square on *La Butte.*

Sacré Coeur. This odd white Byzantine basilica on the heights of Montmartre dominates the skyline as one of the landmarks of Paris Breath-taking view from the terrace.

Place des Vosges. The oldest royal square in Paris still maintains its lovely old houses and quaint atmosphere of the 17th century.

ON THE ILE DE LA CITE

Notre Dame. The famous Gothic Cathedral of Paris. Everyone climbs to the top for the gargoyles and unique view of the heart of the city.

Sainte-Chapelle. A gem of Gothic architecture with the most beautiful stained glass in Paris.

Conciergerie. The historic prison where Marie Antoinette and other victims of the Revolution awaited their execution.

Pont Alexandre III

ON THE ILE ST. LOUIS

This charming and serene island in the city's center is studded with magnificent old mansions and picturesque walks along its quays.

ON THE LEFT BANK

The Eiffel Tower. A miracle of strength and lightness, the most famous symbol of Paris offers the loftiest view of the city and its environs in all directions. Fabulous on a clear day.

The Latin Quarter. The famous student section centered around the old streets near the Sorbonne University.

The Quays. The banks of the Seine offer the perfect place to walk and browse along more than two miles of open-air bookstalls.

Luxembourg Gardens. These lovely informal gardens form the pleasantest park in Paris, a favorite of students and children.

St. Germain-des-Prés. The handsome bell tower of one of the oldest churches in Paris stands near such renowned literary rendezvous as the *Café des Deux Magots*.

The Invalides. Under the handsome golden dome of the Church of the Invalides is the tomb of Napoleon.

Montparnasse. The quarter frequented by artists and writers. Its most celebrated café is the *Dôme*.

The following description of things to see in Paris is designed to help you see as much as possible without retracing steps. The various sights are grouped in neighborhoods or districts according to their nearness to each other. If you ride to the indicated district, you can then walk from one place to the other. Once you have learned how to use the Métro or the buses that radiate everywhere (see Transportation in THINGS TO KNOW), you will have no difficulty in getting to every center of interest described here, even without taxis.

THE ILE DE LA CITE

This lovely island, protected by the two arms of the river, was the small nucleus from which Paris grew. When Caesar conquered Gaul in the first century B.C., the little island was a thriving fishing village inhabited by the *Parisii* tribe. It grew rapidly and became an important trading link in the Roman Empire. After the fall of Rome, the inhabitants called it Paris rather than its Roman name, *Lutetia*. And today Parisians call this history-rich spot "the heart of the city."

Pont Neuf. There are many approaches to the Ile de la Cité, but the best way is to cross from the Left Bank on the Pont Neuf. In spite of its name, this is the oldest (and finest) bridge in Paris, going back to the early 17th century. Where the bridge crosses the island, you will see a fine equestrian statue of Henri IV. This statue has had a curious history, linked, as are most of the landmarks of Paris, to the French Revolution and Napoleon. It stood on the Pont Neuf from 1615 until 1792 when it was melted down to make cannon for the Revolution. A generation later, Napoleon's statue in the Place Vendôme was melted down to make the present statue of Henri IV. (A new one of Napoleon is now back in the Place Vendôme.)

Square du Vert-Galant. Behind the statue you will find steps going down to the river bank. Make this little side trip because it will lead you to the charming little triangular garden known as the Square du Vert-Galant, the Green Gallant being the nickname of the dashing Henri IV. Here at the westernmost tip of the island you will have a marvelous view of the Seine and the Louvre. Above all, it is a very atmospheric and Parisian spot: a place where philosophic men fish all year long and never catch anything; where Sunday painters set up their easels; where lovers meet under the arch of the time-worn bridge.

Place Dauphine. As you go back up the stairs, you will be facing a small park named after the Dauphin, Henri IV's son. The two rose-colored brick buildings at the entrance are still the same as they were in the early 17th century. On one of them is a tablet recording that Mme. Roland lived there. The quiet atmosphere of this square in the heart of Paris makes the pleasant living quarters here very much in demand.

Palais de Justice. Opposite the Place Dauphine you cannot miss the huge sprawling block of buildings that takes up the entire width of the western end of the island, the Palais de Justice. The early kings of France built a royal palace here during the 10th century, which successive kings kept extending. Some of the medieval parts still stand, but with many fires, and restorations in the 18th and 19th centuries, not much remains of the original appearance. During the Revolution, the Courts of Justice were set up here, and the name Palais Royal was changed to Palais de Justice. Today it houses the Civil Law Courts

The Ile de la Cité; Sainte Chapelle and the Place Dauphine

and some departments of the Préfecture de Police—the "Scotland Yard" of Paris. The law courts are open to visitors, and you can see the French lawyers (a surprising number of them are women) in their distinctive gowns. But if your time is limited, the most worth-while things to visit are the infamous prison of the Conciergerie and the lovely Gothic Church of Sainte-Chapelle.

The Conciergerie. Between the last two towers of the palace is the entrance to the Conciergerie. This prison, which took its name from the "concierge" or Master of the King's Household, has more grim associations with the Reign of Terror during the Revolution than any other building in Paris. Condemned prisoners were usually kept here before being sent to the scaffold. Marie-Antoinette, Mme. du Barry, Mme. Roland, Charlotte Corday, who had killed Marat, the poet André Chenier, then finally the Revolutionary leaders Danton and Robespierre, were among the more famous of the thousands who waited here to meet Dr. Guillotine's "philanthropic beheading machine." The Conciergerie is open to the public only on a conducted visit. Among the high points are Marie Antoinette's cell, the Chapel containing orders for the release from prison of Victor Hugo, and the *Salle des Gardes* and *Salle des Gens d'Armes,* two fine Gothic rooms from the ancient palace.

Sainte-Chapelle (Holy Chapel). Even if you have time to see nothing else in the Palais de Justice, a visit to this exquisite chapel would be worth the trip. It is a small church in a poor setting, hidden away in one of the courtyards, but it is a pure gem of Gothic architecture. Louis IX (Saint Louis) had it built in 1246 as a shrine for holy relics, especially the Crown of Thorns and a fragment of the Cross that he had bought from the Emperor of Constantinople at a huge price. During the Revolution the precious relics were almost completely destroyed, and the little that was saved is now part of the Treasury in Notre Dame.

Sainte-Chapelle has two independent chapels, one on top of the other. The entire floor of the lower chapel consists of tombstones of famous people; a crypt-like feeling pervades this starkly beautiful and dim area. In dramatic contrast the upper chapel is bathed in a glory of jewelled light from fifteen tall stained-glass windows. No solid zone of masonry can be seen anywhere. The columns are so slender that the continuity of light is never disturbed, making it look as if the walls were made entirely of stained glass. The stained glass of the Sainte-Chapelle, second only to that of Chartres, is the finest in Paris. Much of it dates from the 13th century, with all the marvelous coloring of that period, and what has been restored has been done with such rare skill that the new blends perfectly with the old. If you have time to examine only one of the windows in detail, look at the great rose at the entrance, which depicts the Apocalypse in wonderful detail.

Marché aux Fleurs (Flower Market). After leaving Sainte-Chapelle, cross the street and you will be in the Marché aux Fleurs. Paris has many flower markets, but this is the largest and best of them. In the morning especially, it presents an incredible variety of flowers and plants beautifully displayed. Every Sunday afternoon it turns into a bird market. Many of Paris' great painters have tried to capture the special flavor of this pleasant and colorful place.

Behind the Marché aux Fleurs looms the massive gray and depressing Hôtel Dieu, the main city hospital. On the Rue de la Cité make a right turn and follow this street for a short block. As so often happens in Paris, there's a surprise around the corner. A few steps away is one of the greatest spiritual and architectural marvels of the world.

Notre Dame de Paris (The Cathedral of Paris). When you step into the spacious esplanade known as the Parvis de Notre Dame, there at the other end stands proud Notre Dame de Paris, its two straight-topped towers tinted gray or rose, depending on the sun. The setting was not always so perfect. Before this area was opened by Napoleon III, it was a clutter of medieval streets, old houses, and little churches crowding up quite close to the Cathedral.

The cornerstone was laid in 1163, and most of the church was finished before 1300. Notre Dame was the product of a fervent tidal wave of faith that swept over France at that time; master architect, lord and commoner, sculptor, merchant, clergy, and king joined in its building. Though work went on well into the 14th century, it has an architectural unity rare in medieval churches, probably because the original plan of the unknown 12th-century architect was respected.

Your first general view of the enormous elevation and width of Notre Dame is not overwhelming; its beautiful proportions and simplicity offer instead a feeling of great, spatial harmony. It rises almost 115 feet, is 157 feet wide, and 425 feet long, and can comfortably hold 9,000 people. On special occasions such as Christmas Mass, or at the Liberation of Paris, it has absorbed as many as 13,000.

To see the outside of Notre Dame it is best to start at the main western facade of the Cathedral. As you face the church, the *Portal of the Virgin* is on the left, the larger *Portal of the Last Judgement* in the center, and the *Portal of Saint Anne* on the right. Take your time studying the exquisite detail of the rich, yet restrained, sculptures which cover almost every inch of the sides and tops of these arched portals. They tell many stories, and the longer you look the more fascinating they become. Above the portals extending over the entire façade is a line of twenty-eight statues of kings from the Old Testament. During the Revolution, these were mistakenly thought to be French kings and pulled down; later they were replaced. Above this gallery of kings are three large windows. In front of the center

The flying buttresses of Notre Dame

one, known as the *Western Rose,* stands a magnificent statue of the *Virgin and Child.* Above the windows is a balustrade from which project those curious gargoyles recognized everywhere as the symbol of Notre Dame, and over all rise the two impressive and finely proportioned towers, the large openings creating an effect of lightness. Notice that no absolute symmetry is preserved anywhere. The towers are of slightly different size, the left (north) tower being slightly wider than its companion to the right.

From the north side, look at the magnificent flying buttresses, which from this spot seem almost suspended in mid-air. Notre Dame was the first to use these bold, yet graceful, supports.

The south or river side, which is bordered by attractive gardens, contains the *Portal of St. Etienne.* Because it opens into the private gardens of the presbytery, a railing surrounds it, and special permission must be obtained to see this door at close range.

Entering the Cathedral, you are engulfed by the special atmosphere created by the huge stained-glass windows, which softly diffuse the light. Of the three great rose windows that alone retain the 13th-century glass, the rich and beautiful *Northern Rose* is the finest, the masterpiece of Jehan de Chelles, one of the greatest stained-glass makers. It is especially breath-taking when the setting sun is behind it.

As you make your way around the Cathedral, you will pass the fourteen chapels which line its sides; the towering nave; the choir, with a lovely 14th-century statue of the Virgin and Child in front of it; the columns in the aisles, with their delicately carved capitals; the impressive rounded main vault; and many other things you may stop to admire. But the most striking thing about the interior is its simplicity. Nothing detracts from the classic line of the nave, the windows, and galleries. This is one of the finest examples of Gothic architecture in the world.

The trip to the towers—the towers which play such a dramatic part in Victor Hugo's "Hunchback of Notre Dame"—is something you should not miss in spite of the 387 steps it takes to climb to the top. The Eiffel Tower and a few other places afford a more lofty view, but nowhere can you get a more intimate look at the center of Paris. Up here you will also have a chance to examine the famous gargoyles on the roof—those grotesque figures of half-human beasts,

Ile de la Cité and Ile St. Louis

birds and devils, each with a different repellent, yet fascinating face.

After you leave the Cathedral, make your way to the Pont St. Louis, the bridge connecting the Cité to the other island in the Seine, the Ile St. Louis. If you turn around just before you cross the river, you will see a new and arresting vista of Notre Dame, with a full view of the magnificent apse and the whole sweep of the flying buttresses.

THE ILE ST. LOUIS

This small and precious island is one of the quietest and most attractive parts of Paris. It is wholly residential, and because of its peaceful riverside charm, the apartments in its spacious 17th- and 18th-century mansions are much sought after. Though it is only a few minutes from Notre Dame, tourists unfortunately seldom find their way here. The Ile St. Louis is one of the most wonderful places in Paris for a leisurely stroll: almost no traffic, surrounded on all sides by delightful quays, and shaded by tall ancient trees. Walking through the streets, you will see fine old mansions, many marked by historical plaques.

The Rue St. Louis, the main street, runs down the entire length of the island, cutting it in two. Halfway down this street is the *Church of St. Louis-en-L'Ile,* interesting mainly for its curious openwork spire and its paintings of the Flemish School. When you reach the tip of the island, make a left turn and you will be on the Quai d'Anjou.

Hôtel de Lauzun and Hôtel Lambert. Here, within a few steps of each other are two splendid 17th-century mansions. The Hôtel de Lauzun, one of the most beautiful houses in Paris, is now owned by the city, and its marvelously decorated rooms are shown on a conducted visit. During the 19th century it was turned into an apartment dwelling, and the writers Gautier and Baudelaire lived there. The Hôtel Lambert, once the home of Voltaire, is not open to the public. But even a look at the outside will tell you why it is considered one of the finest private mansions in France.

Continue on the Quai d'Anjou as far as the Rue des Deux Ponts. Make a left turn here, then cross the bridge called Pont de la Tournelle, which will take you over to the Left Bank. Facing you across the river is the south side of Notre Dame. Even on a rainy day this view is one of the most impressive in Paris.

THE LEFT BANK

A walk along the winding quays of the Left Bank is one of the pleasantest and most Parisian of activities. All along the quays are those famous open-air bookstalls, really a series of long boxes resting on the parapets of the Seine, filled with books, prints, etchings, maps, stamps, coins, and medals. It's harder than it once was to run across a real find, but occasionally a bibliophile still unearths a valuable first edition from the pile of secondhand books. For anyone, however, this is a pleasant place to browse for old prints, maps, and other typically French items that make charming and inexpensive gifts.

THE LATIN QUARTER

The name *Quartier Latin* originally meant simply the place where Latin was spoken. In the early Middle Ages, even before the Sorbonne was established, students came from every country in Europe to study here, and Latin was their common language. The Latin Quarter calls up visions of gay Bohemianism, and, of course, there is still plenty of that left among the students. But mainly this quarter is, as it has been in the past, the center of the intellectual life of France, the home of a great university and of the learned and scientific societies.

Place Saint Michel. This square, dominated by a monumental fountain showing St. Michael slaying the dragon, is where the Boulevard St. Michel begins. The "Boul Mich" is the student's own street and the best introduction to a very lively and historic area. The Sorbonne itself and many of the other buildings which make up the University of Paris are only a few hundred yards away.

St. Julien le Pauvre. About a block east across the Rue du Petit Pont is one of the oldest churches in Paris (built about 1170). It took its odd name from a St. Julien, who was nicknamed "the Poor" because he was always giving away all his money. This small dark church looks more like a little village church than something you would expect to find in Paris. Today it is used for Greek Catholic services. In the ancient catacombs underneath the church are located, of all things, two small night clubs, which feature old French songs. Make a right turn here and walk up the picturesque Rue St. Séverin for one block.

St. Séverin. Rising out of the labyrinth of narrow streets here—looking probably very much the way it did in medieval days—is one of the architectural gems of Paris. Though much restored since the 13th century, St. Séverin has maintained its original simplicity. As in many Gothic churches, the stained-glass windows play an important part in establishing the atmosphere, and the stained glass here is especially beautiful. Some of the windows in the nave tell the story of the murder in Canterbury Cathedral of St. Thomas à Becket.

Musée de Cluny. Going up the Rue St. Jacques, cross the wide Boulevard St. Germain, and turn right at Rue du Sommerard. About fifty yards down the street you will see the Cluny Museum—many people consider it the most attractive museum in Paris. Originally the private residence of the abbots of Cluny, it is one of the rare medieval buildings still existing in Paris. Even the most ordinary things here—the staircases, ceilings, windows, marble fireplaces, and carved doorways —are done with exquisite workmanship. The museum is devoted mainly to French art and crafts of the Middle Ages. (Perhaps one of the nicest things about it is that it is small and selective—almost everything is worth looking at.) There is an especially interesting exhibition called "Life in the Middle Ages," which vividly illustrates the everyday life of nobles and common people. Cluny possesses possibly the finest tapestry in the world. Called *La Dame à la Licorne* (Lady with the Unicorn), it is a fantasy of the Middle Ages—filled with strange beasts, minstrels and crusaders, romantic knights, castles, and a legendary princess.

In the garden of the museum are the ruins of the Roman baths, known as *Les Thermes,* impressive mainly for their enormous size. Here, too, are some other rare relics from Roman days. Look especially at four carved altars from the time of Emperor Tiberius, who reigned during the lifetime of Christ. Sculptures of both Roman and Gallic gods share the same altars, but what a difference in their execution! The Roman gods are dull and uninteresting, while the Gallic gods are small masterpieces of enthusiasm and excitement.

As you leave the Cluny, you are in the heart of the Latin Quarter, with the Sorbonne, the Pantheon, and the Luxembourg Gardens just two blocks away. The central artery of this lively, throbbing students' quarter, the Boulevard St. Michel, is crowded with cafés and little restaurants. You will be struck by the colorful diversity in the appearance of the students, many of them from the Far East, and the amazing number of languages being spoken.

Sorbonne. The main entrance to the Sorbonne is off the little square called Place de la Sorbonne, about two hundred yards from the Cluny Museum. The Sorbonne takes its name from Robert de Sorbon, who founded the first college of the university in 1253. Though today it comprises chiefly the Faculty of Letters and of Sciences, the name Sorbonne is often used for the whole University of Paris. At the main entrance, you will see the Church of the Sorbonne, which contains Richelieu's tomb. It was the powerful Cardinal who, as head of the Sorbonne in the 17th century, decreed that the faculty should owe allegiance neither to Paris nor to France, but only to the Council of the Sorbonne. This, of course, permitted teachers wide freedom, and accounts for much of the independent spirit of the University.

Collège de France. Behind the Sorbonne, at the intersection of the Rue St. Jacques and the Rue des Ecoles, is the Collège de France. Though the most eminent scholars of France teach here, all courses are free and open to the general public. Many Americans take advantage of this opportunity. Even if you don't have time to visit any of the classes, you can catch the flavor of student life by strolling through the courtyards and around the buildings and narrow old side streets; by browsing in the bookstores or sipping a drink in one of the many student cafés. Adjacent to the Collège de France is the Rue St. Jacques. Going uphill on this street, you cannot fail to spot the largest edifice in the Latin Quarter, the Pantheon.

Le Panthéon. Standing on the highest hill of the Left Bank, known as Montagne Ste. Geneviève, it originally housed the church, named for Ste. Geneviève, the patron saint of Paris. During the Revolution it was converted into a Temple of Fame or *Panthéon* to house the illustrious dead. The original church was designed in 1764 by Soufflot, a great architect, with a most ambitious and unusual plan. The proportions are huge: 360 feet long, 270 feet wide, and 272 feet high. Its form of a Greek cross is topped in the center by a magnificent high dome somewhat in the style of St. Paul's Cathedral in London, and lower domes cover the four arms. The architect, it was reported, died of worry and anxiety when the walls were discovered to be sinking. Poor Soufflot would have been even more chagrined had he known that the windows which he had expressly designed to give a feeling of lightness to the building were destined to be filled in when the Revolution decreed a change toward a more massive look. The Pantheon today is impressive, but rather bleak.

There are many paintings and sculptures on the inside, but none of much artistic merit except some fine murals by Puvis de Chavannes showing the life of St. Geneviève. Since the Pantheon became a sort of Westminster Abbey of France a great many of her famous men have been entombed there: among them Voltaire, Jean-Jacques Rousseau, Emile Zola, Victor Hugo, Braille, and Anatole France.

Jardins and Palais du Luxembourg. To get to the Luxembourg Gardens and Palace walk around the Pantheon until you find the Rue Soufflot. Go down that street and cross the Boulevard St. Michel where you will see an entrance to the gardens. The Luxembourg Gardens are the most beautiful in Paris, and by far the most popular. To get the best idea of their scope, walk to the front of the Luxembourg Palace; from there you can see the symmetrical flower beds, always kept freshly blooming, and the long walk which leads to the *Observatoire* almost a mile away. Make sure to see the renowned *Medici Fountain* at the right of the Palace. The circular pool is usually crowded with children sailing toy boats which they can hire by the hour.

The rest of the Luxembourg Gardens is not as formal as this central part, but rather irregular and broken up with shady spots, screened by large trees. The section bordering the Boulevard St. Michel is the favorite walk for students and their girls. Punch and Judy shows given here are so superior that adults, as well as children, crowd to see them.

The Luxembourg Palace was designed in 1615 for Marie de' Medici, the wife of Henri IV. Homesick for her native Florence, she commissioned the architect Salomon de Brosse to create a palace that would be smaller and more intimate than the Louvre. The architect set about transplanting a bit of Tuscany to Paris, with the result that the Luxembourg Palace, while not a direct imitation, is definitely reminiscent of the Pitti Palace in Florence. Now the seat of the upper house of the French Parliament, the palace can be visited only when the chamber is in recess. If you do go, see the library which contains the best of the paintings there: two frescoes by Delacroix.

THE JARDIN DES PLANTES DISTRICT

Arènes de Lutèce (Lutetia Arena). Though the Ile de la Cité is the oldest part of Paris, the rare vestiges from the Roman and early Christian periods in Paris have so far been found exclusively on the Left Bank. Towards the end of the 19th century, a Roman arena was excavated behind the Rue Monge and Rue de Navarre. The arena is not large, but it is classic in its layout; you can see the lines of the amphitheater, the stage, and the complete inside ring.

La Mosquée. About four blocks from the arena, on the Rue Daubenton, you will find the Mosque, built in 1927 to serve the Arab community of Paris. This elaborately decorated white building with its tall minaret and attractive patio is done in the 14th-century Moorish style. Besides the Mosque itself, there are native markets and a Moslem café and restaurants, with strange whining North African music —making it all a veritable bit of the East in the heart of Paris.

Jardin des Plantes (Botanical Gardens). Behind the Mosque, on the other side of the Rue Geoffroy St. Hilaire start the spacious and well-planned Botanical Gardens of Paris, which contain more than ten thousand species of classified plants. Here also is a small zoo and a museum of natural history. (See Museum Guide.) You can find some of the oldest trees in Paris here, including the famous cedar of Lebanon. Particularly on a Sunday afternoon, the park is a favorite promenade area. As you walk down the Botanic Gardens, you cannot help noticing, just behind it, a huge old building with a grandiose dome. This is La Salpetrière, once an arsenal, and now a hospital. Its immense size makes it a Paris landmark, but it hardly merits any closer inspection.

Manufactures Nationales de Tapisseries des Gobelins. Somewhat out of the way, but well worth visiting, is the Gobelins tapestry factory at 42 Avenue des Gobelins, near the Place d'Italie. Visitors who find their way here rate it one of the most fascinating exhibits in Paris. The world-famous tapestries have been made here since the early 15th century, and they are still made in the same way. Nothing mechanical has been added; the craftsmen still use the ancient looms and other equipment. It is astonishing to watch their painstaking work and realize that each man produces no more than 1½ square feet of tapestry per month. These workshops are open to the public on Wednesday, Thursday, and Friday afternoons.

MONTPARNASSE AND VICINITY

Near enough to the Latin Quarter to share in its Bohemian life, Montparnasse is also far enough away to have a distinct life and quality of its own. After World War I, Picasso, Braque, Picabia, and other "unfashionable" painters of the time moved to this quarter to work because Montmartre was becoming too touristy. They were soon followed by a swarm of young painters and students, and an international art colony came into being. In the twenties, the larger cafés and brasseries like the original *Rotonde* and the *Dôme,* at the intersection of the Boulevards Raspail and Montparnasse, became the favorite haunts of such American expatriate writers as Hemingway, Gertrude Stein, and Henry Miller. Today they still attract a large and colorful following and are pleasant places to stop and relax and watch Parisians of all sorts amble by.

At the corner of the same intersection stands an unusual bronze statue of Balzac, swathed in a large cape. It was commissioned as long ago as 1898 by the French Literary Society. But many of the members were shocked at the sculptor's interpretation, and a typical French controversy raged over it for more than forty years. It was not until 1939, by which time the statue had already been universally acclaimed as one of Rodin's masterpieces, that it was finally set up in the square.

A modern controversy now surrounds the 210-meter tall Tour Maine-Montparnasse, completed in 1974. A shopping center with 80 stores on the ground level, a fine restaurant with a superb view, and a convenient heliport do not, in the eyes of most Parisians, prevent this building from being anything but an affront to the architectural harmony of their city.

Place Furstenburg

The Catacombs. The main entrance to these unusual catacombs is on the Place Denfert-Rochereau. Originally a series of vast underground quarries that had been worked as far back as Roman times, in the 18th century they began to be used for storage of human bones removed from abandoned cemeteries. These human bones and skulls are now piled up along the walls as decoration. A candle-lit visit here is a memorable experience of the weird and macabre, but definitely not for the squeamish. During the last war the French Underground used the catacombs as one of its headquarters and from there directed operations for the Liberation of Paris.

Val-de-Grâce. At 277 bis Rue St. Jacques are some 17th-century buildings made up of a handsome church and the old Abbaye du Val-de-Grâce, originally a convent for Benedictine nuns. Both were erected by Anne of Austria in thanksgiving for the birth of Louis XIV, an event for which she had waited twenty-three years. The church has a celebrated, heavily ornate dome about which the Parisians say, "If you wish to understand France, you must learn to like Camembert cheese, the Pont Neuf, and the dome of Val-de-Grâce." Inside there is a famous fresco by Mignard and brilliant marble mosaic pavings.

ST. GERMAIN-DES-PRES DISTRICT

This entire quarter is a very old and fascinating one. If you wander off the Boulevard St. Germain in the direction of the Seine you will find that this is the realm of antiquity—there are over a hundred antique shops here. The side streets are also crowded with art galleries, bookstores, charming little hotels, and old houses. The heart of this Left Bank quarter is the *Place St. Germain-des-Prés* where the famous so-called "existentialist" cafés—the *Deux Magots,* the *Café de Flore*, and the *Brasserie Lipp*—are situated. Though these cafés gained added prominence when the writers Jean-Paul Sartre and Simone de Beauvoir frequented them after the war, they have been enjoying the patronage of publishers and writers for more than fifty years. St. Germain-des-Prés has become a favorite spot for foreigners, particularly Americans, and if you sit there long enough you are bound to recognize a friend from home or some well-known personality. Many of the famous Left Bank *caves* (cellar night clubs), like the *Vieux Colombier* are also located in this quarter.

Church of St. Germain-des-Prés. The famous ancient church is renowned for its Romanesque tower, beautifully simple and harmonious, dating from 1020. St. Germain-des-Prés goes back to the 6th century, when King Childeberth, son of the first Christian king of France, returned from victories in Spain with precious holy objects and built a church and abbey to house them. Norman invasions destroyed St. Germain-des-Prés four times, but each time it was rebuilt and fortified more heavily, so that by the 13th-century high walls surrounded the entire church. Today it still bears the massive look of a medieval fortress.

The interior is unusual in its combination of Romanesque style in the nave with early Gothic in the choir. You can see the styles merging in the windows of the chapels: the lower ones are still rounded Romanesque while the upper ones are pointed Gothic. The marble columns date from the 6th century. Notice the imaginative capitals here, decorated with human figures, animals, birds, and harpies.

The Place Furstenberg and Balzac's Print Shop. Immediately behind the Church of St. Germain-des-Prés you will discover some of the most charming little streets in Paris. Off the Rue de l'Abbaye is the enchanting Place Furstenberg, which looks even prettier at night when its old-fashioned lighting fixtures illuminate the serene square and the magnolia trees in the center. At No. 6, the painter Delacroix had his studio. It has been turned into a museum, open daily 9:45 A.M. to 5:15 P.M. Closed Tuesdays.

Nearby, at 17 Rue Visconti is the building where Balzac used to run his printing plant. The novelist was singularly unsuccessful when he first started to write, and thinking he had quite a head for business, he borrowed money for a printing press. This, like most of the other business ventures he undertook in his youth, ended in failure. This was fortunate because he then went back to writing, turning out one masterpiece after another in order to pay off his debts.

Ecole des Beaux Arts. The Rue Visconti runs into the Rue Bonaparte. At No. 14 you will see the gate and courtyard of the Ecole des Beaux Arts, the world-famous school for painters, sculptors, and architects. The courtyard is a sort of open-air architectural museum, and inside hang paintings by famous former students. Many of the world's great architects, particularly Americans, have studied here, as well as most of the well-known French painters. The cynics say that they study at the Beaux Arts only to fly in the face of their training as soon as they get out. To the public the school is best known for the wild and original costumes of the students' annual ball, *Bal* *des Quatres Arts,* which everyone tries to crash, and few succeed.

L'Institut de France. At the foot of the Rue Bonaparte, where it meets the quay, stands a distinguished 17th-century building with a curved façade and a notable cupola. The interior courtyards and surrounding pavilions are particularly handsome. This is the home of the five French Academies of the Institut de France: the *Académie Française,* the *Académie des Inscriptions et Belles Lettres,* the *Académie des Sciences Morales et Politiques,* the *Académie des Sciences,* and the *Académie des Beaux Arts.* Its some 225 members are generally considered the most distinguished scholars in France. When most people refer to an "academician," however, they mean a member of the first of these academies, the Académie Française, the literary society restricted to the forty "immortals," who edit the dictionary of the French language, lay down rules of grammar, and authorize the admission of new words into the language. Their chief job lately seems to be that of trying to keep out American words.

St. Sulpice. Though the Place St. Sulpice is hardly more than two hundred yards from St. Germain-des-Prés, a completely different atmosphere pervades this area. Too small to be a quarter in itself, it nonetheless conveys that impression. If you sit down for a while by the fountain on the quiet square in front of the church of St. Sulpice, you will get that feeling so unique to some parts of Paris, that you actually are in a small French town.

The huge church, the second largest in Paris and the most important one on the Left Bank, was built during the 17th and 18th centuries. Its façade, by the Italian architect Servandoni, consists of a majestic portico in which Ionic columns are superimposed on Doric. Another striking effect is contributed by the two dissimilar towers, the north tower sixteen feet higher than the southern one. The interior, on the other hand, is very much in the classical tradition. As you enter, the first chapel on the right is adorned by magnificent Delacroix frescoes, especially the remarkable one of *Jacob Wrestling with the Angel.* In the Chapel of the Virgin, look for Van Loo's *Scenes from the Life of the Virgin,* and some lovely statues by Bouchardon near the choir.

LES INVALIDES DISTRICT

Unlike the crowded, crooked streets of St. Germain-des-Prés, this quarter is one of wide open spaces. The monuments here— among them the Invalides, the Rodin Museum, and, of course, the Eiffel Tower—have splendid settings and large esplanades.

Tour Eiffel. When the Eiffel Tower was first built for the Paris

World Fair of 1889, it was the butt of many jokes and criticism because of its lack of beauty. Called everything from a curiosity to a monstrosity, it was almost torn down ten years after the fair. But today everyone regards it with sentimental affection. It is the best-known landmark of Paris, as much a part of it as the Seine. Structurally, Alexandre Eiffel's Tower is a brilliant engineering feat: its lightness and strength are such that the pressure per square inch that it exerts on the ground is no greater than the pressure per square inch of a chair with an average man in it. At 985 feet it was, until the erection of the Chrysler Building in New York, the tallest structure in the world.

The view from the top is truly fabulous. All of Paris and the neighboring towns within a forty-mile radius can be seen on a clear day, especially at the hour before sunset. On both the first and second landings are fine restaurants, and eating there with the panorama of Paris spread out before you is a uniquely pleasurable experience. A word of caution—don't visit the tower on a misty, windy, or very cold day.

Champs de Mars. The Eiffel Tower stands on the north end of the vast parade grounds known as the Champs de Mars that stretch all the way south more than half a mile to the *Ecole Militaire*. Both were designed by the great architect Gabriel, who laid out the Place de la Concorde. The Champs de Mars has many historical associations: during the Revolution it became the scene of some of the most violent riots and celebrations; the first balloon ascents took place here; and it was on this field that Captain Dreyfus was degraded in a public ceremony in 1894. Today its landscaped grounds are used mainly as a park.

Ecole Militaire (Military Academy). Gabriel's handsome 18th-century school looks more like a palace than a military academy. Designed to provide officer's training for the sons of poor aristocrats, it was later opened to superior students from provincial academies. One of these was its most famous graduate, Napoleon Bonaparte. His final report card carried the notation: "Will go far, if circumstances permit." The most impressive single feature of these surprisingly magnificent barracks is the central pavilion with its pleasing Corinthian columns and quadrangular dome. The building is now used as the Staff College of the Army and the Air Force.

Les Invalides. When the Invalides was started by Louis XIV in 1671, it was used as a home for some seven thousand disabled soldiers, and during the time of Napoleon it served the same purpose. Today, however, only a very small section houses some hundred wounded war veterans. The rest is used for numerous army offices and the huge War Museum. (See Museum Guide.) The most notable sights are Napoleon's tomb and the dome by Mansart.

It is best to approach the Invalides from the north or river side, where the open sweep of the esplanade will let you observe all of the simple and beautiful façade (nearly seven hundred feet long). Before passing through the imposing central portal, look for the statue of Louis XIV on horseback, surrounded by two figures, Justice and Prudence. In the *Cour d'Honneur* on the other side of the portal are historical trophies decorating the fine gable windows.

Directly across this courtyard is the entrance to the *Eglise St. Louis*, called the "Soldier's Church" because of the numerous great soldiers buried here, among them General Giraud of North Africa fame and General Leclerc, whose tank corps was the first to enter Paris during the Liberation. The flags and standards hanging from the ceiling and walls of the church colorfully recall France's military glories. Here too is *Napoleon's Chapel*, especially interesting for his death mask and the slabs that marked his grave at St. Helena.

Behind Napoleon's Chapel you will find the *Eglise du Dôme*, the church famous for its great dome and for Napoleon's tomb. As the dome is unquestionably one of the most beautiful sights in Paris, it is worth while to walk over to the Place Vauban (the south side) where it stands out in all its splendor. The high point, of course, is the central tomb of Napoleon I. As you descend into the crypt, there is an inscription with Napoleon's moving words: "I want my body to rest by the banks of the Seine, among the French people whom I loved so dearly." The tomb, designed by Visconti, lies in a slightly sunken circular well, directly under the great dome. Of red porphyry, a very rare stone, it rests on a base of green granite; six coffins, contained one within the other, protect the body of Napoleon. Surrounding the tomb are the Emperor's trophies and flags and twelve colossal statues, symbolic of his twelve major military victories. Considerable controversy has raged over the artistic merits of this tomb but, whether you like it or not, its power and unusual execution certainly leave an unforgettable impression.

Musée Rodin. On the corner of the Boulevard des Invalides and the Rue de Varenne stands one of Gabriel's magnificent early 18th-century mansions. When the French government purchased this *Hôtel Biron* in 1910, the great sculptor made a special deal: he would leave his work to the French people provided the government let him have the use of the house until his death. It was a mutually happy arrangement, and Rodin's work can be seen here in a perfect setting. You will find such famous statues as *The Thinker* (set in a lovely garden, with one thousand varieties of roses), *The Gates of Hell, Eve, The Kiss, Balzac, Victor Hugo,* and many others. Some of these statues are tastefully arranged throughout the large and beautiful gardens, many more inside the house. There you will also find a series of Rodin drawings and an interesting collection of Impressionist paintings including *Le Père Tanguy,* one of Van Gogh's masterpieces. The Ro-

Palais de Chaillot, directly across the Seine from the Eiffel Tower

din Museum is an unusually informal kind of museum, preferred by many to the larger ones.

Palais Bourbon. Facing the Place de la Concorde from the other side of the Seine is the Palais Bourbon, an impressive building with a portico of great Corinthian columns. The most outstanding of the many statues here is the one of *Justice* by Houdon, at the top of the steps. Once the private residence of the Duchess of Bourbon, illegitimate daughter of Louis XIV, it was later bought by the government and considerably enlarged Napoleon had the present classic façade designed to harmonize with the Place de la Concorde and the Corinthian porch of the Madeleine. Today it is the seat of the French National Assembly.

THE RIGHT BANK

Place du Châtelet. One of the busiest squares in Paris, it is named after the old fortress, Le Grand Châtelet, which used to stand here by the Seine to protect the northern approach to the Ile de la Cité. One of Paris' largest theatres, the *Théâtre du Châtelet* now occupies the west side of the square, and opposite is a somewhat smaller theater, the *Théâtre de la Ville*. The fountain in the center, called the *Fontaine du Palmier*, is a memorial to the great victories of Napoleon.

Tour St. Jacques (Tower of St. Jacques). Just behind the Châtelet and away from the river rises the solitary spire of St. Jacques. Though the tower is all that remains of the 16th-century church that stood here before the Revolution, its eloquent late Gothic style bears witness to the good taste of King François I, under whose auspices it was constructed. When the Rue de Rivoli was being extended, it was suggested that the tower be demolished to make room for a new esplanade. The Parisians, who love the monuments of their beautiful city, were outraged. Victor Hugo, who championed not only the arts but popular sentiment, summed up the protest thus: "Destroy the Tour St. Jacques? *Never!* Destroy the architect who suggested it." The tower is now used as a meteorological observatory.

St. Gervais-St. Protais. Behind the Hôtel de Ville in the midst of an old elm-tree garden is an unusual church dedicated to two Roman martyrs, St. Gervais and St. Protais. Started in the late 15th century, the classic façade was the first attempt in France to combine the Doric, Ionic, and Corinthian orders into one structure. The lofty interior, in pure late Gothic style, has some fine stained-glass windows and numerous Renaissance works of art, including a painting by Perugino. Notice especially the exquisite *Chapel of the Virgin* and the fine carvings in the *Chapelle Dorée.* The church has a famous old organ which has been played here for almost two centuries by that illustrious dynasty of organists, the Couperin family. Its choir is rated among the most remarkable in France.

Archives Nationales. On the corner of the Rue des Archives and the Rue des Francs-Bourgeois stand the two buildings of the Archives Nationales. They contain the most important historical documents of France, dating from earliest Merovingian times of the 6th century to World War II. A visit to the Archives is made even more inviting since they are housed in the *Hôtel de Soubise* and *Hôtel de Rohan,* two superb mansions built about 1700. The interiors are magnificently maintained, and the decorations of these rooms represent the best talent of the 18th century. Some fine paintings by Boucher, Natoire, and Van Loo further enhance these lush surroundings. In the Hôtel de Soubise you will find the interesting *Musée de l'Histoire de France,* which gives an excellent picture of the various historical periods by means of authentic documents. Among the letters of French royalty and foreign personalities are several by Franklin and Washington.

Les Halles (The Central Market). Most of the commercial activity that made Les Halles one of the most famous marketplaces in the world has recently been transferred to a new location on the southern outskirts of Paris. The old market area has thus lost most of its interest, but a few of the well-known restaurants, specializing in onion soup, *tripes à la mode de Caen,* and snails, are still in operation. They do not, however, remain open throughout the night, as they did during the heyday of the market, and now should be visited during the regular dinner hour rather than at three in the morning.

St. Eustache. Facing Les Halles at the corner of the Rue Montmartre and the Rue Coquillière is the large church of St. Eustache, sometimes called *Notre Dame des Halles* because its plan resembles that of the more famous Cathedral. Though laid out along Gothic lines during the 16th century, its decoration is in the best Renaissance tradition. Outstanding examples are the handsomely carved doorways of the transept, the fine stained-glass windows, the paintings, and large frescoes. The soaring height of the nave and the impressive richness of the decorations lead many people to rank St. Eustache as the second most beautiful church in Paris. It is also famous for its music; the services at midnight mass on Christmas Eve and on Good Friday are considered great musical events.

Place de la République. Seven important thoroughfares end in the Place de la République, whose enormous size gives the impression that it must represent some glorious victory. And this is perhaps the only *place* in Paris of which this is not true. It is strictly the work of the sly and brilliant Baron Haussmann, who was not only the city planner for Napoleon III, but also his Chief of Police. Ever aware of the revolutionary spirit alive in Paris in the 1850's, Haussmann decided to keep the populace in order by building wide boulevards right through a slum district, and to have these boulevards all terminate in large central squares. On the Place de la République he erected barracks holding some two thousand men ready to quell any revolt. The monument in the center, dedicated to the Republic of France, is not much artistically, but its heroic size harmonizes with the square. Nowadays the Place de la République is a favorite rallying point for political demonstrations.

FROM THE PLACE DE LA BASTILLE TO THE BOIS DE VINCENNES

Place de la Bastille. The word *bastille* means bastion or fortification, and that was exactly what Charles V ordered constructed here in 1370. By the time of Louis XIII the Bastille had become a prison for political offenders. Among the political figures imprisoned here were the mysterious "Man in the Iron Mask," the Minister of Finance, Fouquet, Cagliostro and his wife, the Cardinal de Rohan, and Voltaire.

When the Bastille was stormed on July 14, 1789, it was no longer an important prison. In fact, much to the Revolutionaries' surprise, only seven prisoners were found. But the Bastille had become a symbol of royal oppression and injustice, and the attack on it was the trigger action which set off the French Revolution. It is the 14th of July which the French keep as their great national holiday. So thor-

Historic Paris comes alive in the collections of the Musée Carnavalet   *Les Invalides*

oughly did the angry mob raze this formidable fortress that, with the exception of a few foundation stones, (which can be seen in the Bastille Métro station), nothing else was left. On the Boulevard Henri IV, where the prison once stood, its site is now traced by a line of white paving blocks. The lofty column crowned by a figure of Liberty in the center of the square is known as the *Colonne de Juillet,* or July Column. Strangely enough, it does not commemorate Bastille Day, but the July Revolution of 1830

Place des Vosges. One of the most enchanting and least known of the city's picturesque squares is the Place des Vosges—about two blocks from the Bastille. It was created for Henri IV in 1605 as the first royal square, and the middle building of the south side was designed to be Henri IV's own residence. Unfortunately he was murdered before he could move in. A unique feature of the square resulted from the King's order that "all buildings were to be built symmetrically and of the same height." Today the square is still surrounded by the original harmonious rose-colored brick buildings with their elegant white stone arcades. A walk in this dream-like place is a return to the 17th century. Many famous people lived here, among them, Mme. de Sévigné, Cardinal Richelieu, and the writers Gautier, Daudet, and Victor Hugo. Victor Hugo's house at No. 6 has been converted into a public museum.

Musée Carnavalet. Near the same square, at the corner of the Rue Francs-Bourgeois and des Rue de Sévigné, one of the magnificent old mansions is now a museum illustrating the history of Paris from the time of Henri IV to the present. It is not so much a formal museum as a storehouse of personal mementos of the city. The Paris of Louis XIV, the Regency, and, above all, of the 18th century comes to life in these exhibitions. Be sure to look at the models of old Paris, which give an illuminating picture of the city and its transformations through the ages. Especially fascinating are those rooms which dramatically re-create a particular scene of bygone times by using a famous personality as its central theme.

Père Lachaise Cemetery. At the end of the Avenue de la République, on a high hill, is the city's largest and most famous cemetery, going back to the Middle Ages. Unlike other burial grounds, Père Lachaise is exempt from the usual mournful atmosphere. It is a place of serene beauty and great historic interest. So many of France's celebrated dead are buried here that it has more the air of a vast outdoor sculpture gallery than a cemetery. Among the most admired monuments are the famous one of the 12th-century lovers Abélard and Héloïse, lying side by side under a Gothic canopy; the arresting modern tomb of Oscar Wilde by Jacob Epstein; and Gertrude Stein's gravestone, a masterpiece of dignity and absolute simplicity. The famous people buried here are far too numerous to begin to list, but among the most noteworthy monuments are those to La Fontaine, Molière, Balzac the artists Daumier, Ingres, Delacroix, and Corot; and the composers Rossini, Chopin, and Bizet.

Bois de Vincennes (Forest of Vincennes). About two miles southeast of Père Lachaise is the wonderful Bois de Vincennes, a delightful place to spend a relaxed Sunday afternoon. It has, among other features, a spacious forest, a modern zoo, and an ancient castle. This zoo, one of the finest in Europe, has been specially designed so that the wild animals have more than the usual freedom and space and are not caged, but separated from the spectators by wide moats. Most of the animals live in an atmosphere that recalls their original habitat—an authentic jungle, an African plain, or a rocky mountain setting.

The most interesting feature of the vast and majestic *Château de Vincennes,* is the 14th-century fortified tower known as "The Keep." (It is now a historical museum, open daily except Tuesday.) In the 17th century the Keep began to be used as a dungeon, but long before that, in 1422, the English king Henry V, victor of the great battle of Agincourt, fell ill and died here in the royal bedchamber—just seven weeks before he would have succeeded Charles VI as King of France. Guided tours at 10 and 11:15 A.M., 1:30, 2:30, 3:30 and 4:30 P.M. Closed Tuesday.

THE LOUVRE AND SURROUNDINGS

St. Germain l'Auxerrois. Just east of the Louvre, on the Place du Louvre, stands St. Germain l'Auxerrois, a church with a striking blending of styles: the 12th-century bell tower is Romanesque, the choir and the apse are Gothic, while the north doorway is in the Renaissance tradition. When the Louvre was the royal palace, this church was used by the kings of France as the royal chapel, and a small gallery reserved for them is still there. It was the bells of St. Germain l'Auxerrois that gave the signal for the bloody massacre of St. Bartholomew. On the second Sunday of every month a unique mass is celebrated here—for the souls of departed poets.

The Louvre. The Louvre is the largest museum in the world. Through its unsurpassed collection you could acquire a complete education in the history of art, but anyone who tries to "do" its more than two miles of galleries in a day will acquire only sore feet and bleary eyes. The Louvre is divided into six distinct sections, each of which is really a museum in itself: Egyptian Antiquities, Greek and Roman Antiquities, Oriental Antiquities, Sculpture of the Middle Ages and Renaissance, Art Objects, and Paintings. Even to glance at all the things here would take at least two or three separate visits. You will get the most out of your visits if you concentrate on the two or three sections that appeal to you most.

The Louvre and the Arc de Triomphe du Carroussel

Visitors who are in Paris only for a few days can see most of the major treasures of the Louvre without indigestion *if* they strictly limit themselves to the high spots. The following tour takes in the high spots, but as the Louvre is currently undergoing extensive re-decoration and reorganization, they may not always be located as indicated here. One final word of advice: since the Louvre is a must for every tourist, the crowds invading the halls, especially in the summer months, can be overwhelming. To get a head start on the crush, be there promptly at 9:45 in the morning when the gates open.

To begin this high-spot tour take the entrance known as the *Porte La Trémoille* and begin with a visit to the Sculptures of the Middle Ages and Renaissance. After you reach the end of the first hall, with its many fine examples of medieval French sculpture, turn right and walk straight through to the last room, the Salle Michel-Ange. Here you will find two great works of art: Michelangelo's powerful and tragic *The Slaves*, and Jean Boulogne's marvelously airy *Mercury*. Unfortunately many rooms in the Louvre's sculpture section are closed at the moment for remodelling, and their treasures temporarily hidden from the public eye.

After you have looked at the works in sculpture rooms, walk over to the entrance called *Porte Denon,* which will take you to the main part of this tour. On your left you will see the *Winged Victory* (Nike of Samothrace) superbly set in its own niche at the top of the wide staircase. Take your time over this magnificent Hellenistic statue from the 2nd century B.C. It is surely one of the greatest masterpieces of all time.

If you walk past the left side of the staircase and straight ahead, you will be in that section called Greek and Roman Antiquities, where you will find the most popular statue in the museum, the *Venus de Milo*. Like the Winged Victory this famous statue also dates from the 2nd century B.C. and is beautifully displayed. As you cross over to the other side and slowly walk back, you will be passing sculptures from the 4th and 5th centuries. At the end of this hall is the Salle du Parthénon, where fragments from that most famous temple of the 5th century B.C. are kept. These sculptures represent the high point of Greek art. Turn right and continue straight down till you come to the Salle des Cariatides. This room which is in the process of being re-arranged, contains some world-renowned

Hellenistic sculptures of the many Greek gods, including the much reproduced *Artemis the Huntress*, and the charming *Faun with Child*, known officially as *Silenus and Dionysus.*

Return the.way you came to the Winged Victory and ascend the staircase here. On the second floor, make a right turn which will bring you into the handsome room decorated with the glorious frescoes of Botticelli. Returning to the staircase, this time make a left turn and, at the top on the right you will see another magnificent fresco by Fra Angelico. Opposite this fresco is the Salle de Sept Mètres, one of the finest exhibition halls in the Louvre, containing masterpieces by Rembrandt and Franz Hals. Among these is the famous *Self Portrait* showing Rembrandt in a beret and wearing a gold chain, his portrait of *Hendrikje Stoffels*, and the vivacious *Gypsy Girl* by Hals.

At the end of this room turn right to enter the Grande Galerie, the largest of all the exhibition halls. The first two-thirds of this tremendously long room are occupied by paintings of 17th and 18th century French masters: Poussin, Lorrain, de la Tour, Fragonard and Watteau, to name only a few. The last third of the Grande Galerie features the Italian artists of the primitive period and early Renaissance. Among the gems of the collection are Giotto's *St. Francis of Assisi*, Fra Angelico's splendid *Coronation of the Virgin*, and Uccello's spirited *Battle of San Romano.*

Not quite half-way down this great exhibition hall is a smaller room to the right, known as the Salle des Etats. It is here that you will find three magnificent Leonardo paintings. The most famous of the three and the most visited picture in the Louvre is, of course, the *Mona Lisa.* But the other two, *Virgin of the Rocks* and *Virgin and Child with St. Anne* are just as exciting. Notice how the faint, haunting smile of St. Anne resembles that of the Mona Lisa. As you walk through this room, which is filled with great Italian Renaissance paintings, look particularly for *La Belle Jardinière*, one of the loveliest of all Raphael's pictures, Titian's dramatic *Entombment*, as well as some superb creations by Correggio, Tinteretto and Veronese.

Going back to the Grande Galerie, you will see the entrance to the Salle Van Dyck, which contains Van Dyck's famous *Portrait of Charles I,* as well as some other important paintings including Rubens' glowing family portrait of his second wife, *Helen Fourment and Children.*

The Galerie Medicis, which immediately follows the Salle Van Dyck has a superb collection of twenty-one Rubens masterpieces. In the small alcoves (called cabinets) on either side of this gallery are gems from Flemish, Dutch, German, and French painters. Look particularly for Dürer's *Self Portrait* and Holbein's *Anne of Cleves.* Other works include paintings by Brueghel, Memling, Bosch, Mabuse, and one of the rare and lovely paintings by Vermeer, *The Lacemaker.* These alcoves contain some of the finest paintings in the Louvre, and it is fantastic to see so many masterpieces crammed into such a small space.

After the Galerie Medicis come the 17th and 18th century Italian masters. Keep your eyes open for Guardi's beautifully delicate scenes of Venice, and Tiepolo's magnificent allegory, *The Triumph of Religion.*

The very last gallery you come to houses the great Spanish painters. Velasquez, Zurbarán and Murillo are well represented, but make a special point of seeing Goya's extraordinary *Lady with a Fan,* and El Greco's powerful *Crucifixion.*

Some fine paintings of the 18th century are located on the third floor in the Salles de la Colonnade. To get there, retrace your steps to the staircase near the Winged Victory. Continue straight ahead, through the galleries of Egyptian Antiquities, and near the end of that gallery, on your right, you will find a small staircase which will take you up to the Salles de la Colonnade. The exhibits in these rooms feature the French, English, Spanish, and Italian schools. Here you will find Gainsborough's *Conversation in a Park,* Whistler's famous portrait of his mother, Boucher's *Diana Resting After the Bath,* Ingres' *Bathers* and many other important works by Lawrence, Reynolds, Chardin, Longhi, Greuze, and other masters of the 18th century.

The Louvre Building. The Louvre is not only the largest museum in the world but one of the largest and most magnificent of palaces. In the 16th century François I had the old fortress that had stood on the Louvre site since 1200 razed and a majestic Renaissance palace built in its place. Catherine de' Medici, widow of King Henri II, also liked this location and had another palace built for herself in the Tuileries, quite close to the Louvre. By the end of the 16th century the two palaces were linked by what is now the main exhibition hall for paintings, the Grande Galerie.

The construction of the finest part of the Louvre Palace, the handsome *Cour Carrée* (Square Court) was begun by Louis the XIV, continued by Napoleon I, and finally completed by Napoleon III. During the Commune riots in 1871 the Tuileries Palace and the galleries linking the two palaces were burnt down. Shortly afterward, the galleries (but not the Tuileries Palace) were rebuilt and the rest of the modern part of the Louvre Palace finished. All in all, its construction went on for three centuries. Seen in its entirety the Louvre looks magnificently impressive. However, the details of the later sections are heavily ornate and of rather mediocre workmanship. If you observe the carving, it is not hard to discern the difference between the new and the distinctly superior early craftsmanship. By far the purest and best construction is the marvelous western façade of the Cour Carrée.

Arc de Triomphe du Carroussel. Behind the Louvre is the Roman-style triumphal arch built by Napoleon in celebration of his victorious campaigns of 1805. As you stand under the arch, one of those wonderful vistas of Paris, *la Voie Triomphale,* stretches out before you: the Tuileries Gardens, the Place de la Concorde, and the sweep of the Champs-Elysées all the way up to the gigantic Arc de Triomphe at the Etoile. This is no accident, but an example of the superb city planning which has made Paris the beautiful city it is today.

Jardin des Tuileries (The Tuileries Gardens). Directly behind the Louvre are the beautiful Tuileries, laid out by Le Nôtre in the 17th century and hardly changed to this day. Though the Tuileries are symmetrical formal gardens, they are anything but severe; their openness and spacious views have lightness and charm. And they are a very lively part of Paris, the shady central avenue always filled with strollers enjoying the new displays in the flower beds as they go back and forth from work.

At the end of these gardens and behind the large octangular pool where children sail toy boats, are two handsome museums. The one on the left (as you face the Place de la Concorde) is known as the *Orangerie,* the other, the *Jeu de Paume.* There are some fine statues between these buildings, especially Maillol's *Femme Couchée* in front of the Orangerie. This museum has been remodeled and now contains a fine collection of Impressionist paintings.

Musée du Jeu de Paume. The great Impressionist and Post-Impressionist paintings of the Louvre are now in the Jeu de Paume Museum. This is a superb collection not to be missed by anyone at all interested in modern art. Many brilliant Impressionist masterpieces are on exhibition, including *Le Moulin de la Galette* by Renoir, *The Circus* by Seurat, *Room at Arles* by Van Gogh, *L'Estaque* by Cézanne, and other great paintings by Manet, Degas, Monet, Pissarro, Sisley, Toulouse-Lautrec, and Gauguin. The paintings are admirably arranged in special groups, with illuminating explanations of the methods and techniques of Impressionism.

The Venus de Milo, The Winged Victory, and their home, the Louvre

FROM THE RUE DE RIVOLI TO THE PALAIS ROYALE

Near the Place de la Concorde is the beginning of one of the live-liest and longest thoroughfares in Paris, the *Rue de Rivoli*. Its west-ern end, built in uniform design with covered arcades and balconies, has elegant shops and fine hotels, while the eastern end is a working-class district. Walk along the Rue de Rivoli from the Place de la Con-corde until you reach the Rue de Castiglione—another street for the shopper's delight. Turning left here two short blocks will lead you right into the fabulous Place Vendôme.

Place Vendôme.   One of the architectural beauty spots of Paris, the Place Vendôme was designed for Louis XIV by the brilliant Mansart at the end of the 17th century. To guard its permanent beauty, Man-sart drew up a contract which forbade any future architectural changes. Most of the handsome old buildings are today used for com-mercial purposes—mainly for banks, de luxe businesses, and the in-ternationally famous Ritz Hotel—but the unity of the façades has remained remarkably unchanged.

The history of the statue in the middle of the Place Vendôme, however, is almost as varied as the history of Paris itself. The square was at first adorned with a statue of Louis XIV that was, of course, promptly knocked down during the Revolution. In 1812 a tall col-umn, an imitation of Trajan's column in Rome, with bands of bronze melted down from the cannons captured at Austerlitz and topped with Napoleon dressed as a Roman Caesar, was set up. After the Emperor's defeat, his statue was replaced by one of Henri IV. When Napoleon returned from Elba, Henri IV was pulled down and ex-changed for a gigantic fleur-de-lys. Later a different statue of Bona-parte, this time in his French uniform, was placed on the top. During the riots of 1871 the angry populace pulled down the statue and the entire column. Finally the column was restored and crowned with a copy of the original statue of Napoleon, complete with Roman toga and laurel wreath.

St. Roch.   At the corner of the Rue St. Honoré and the Rue St. Roch stands the Baroque 17th-century church of St. Roch. Because of a hill on the site, it has a curious construction, the nave running north-south, instead of the traditional east-west. There is an unusually fine collection of paintings and sculptures of the 17th and 18th centuries in the church. It was on the steps of St. Roch that the young Bona-parte first gained fame as a leader. October 5, 1795, is remembered as the day that Napoleon, until then an obscure officer, distinguished himself by crushing a serious rebellion with his celebrated "whiff of grapeshot." Marks of the bullets fired by the opposing royalists can still be seen on the front of the church.

Palais Royal.   The Rue St. Honoré leads into the Place du Théâtre Français, where you will find the famous theater by that name. Be-hind the theater lies the peaceful and immensely pleasing garden square of the Palais Royal. The palace itself was originally built for, and named after, Cardinal Richelieu. When he willed it to Louis XIII, it was renamed Palais Royal, but the royal family preferred to live in the Louvre. (It is now occupied by various government offices.) When Parisians refer to the Palais Royal, however, they mean that uniform row of 18th-century houses with arcades of old shops surrounding the large palace garden on three sides. This forms a charming, quiet retreat in the center of the city. The novelist Colette lived here until her death in 1954, and back in 1823 John Howard Payne wrote "Home Sweet Home" in one of these apartments. It is especially pleasant to walk through the gardens at night when its arcades are lit with soft dim lights and the atmosphere seems far removed from the 20th century.

FROM THE OPERA TO THE PLACE DE LA CONCORDE

Les Grands Boulevards. These boulevards extending in a semi-circular curve from the Madeleine to the Place de la Bastille follow the line of the medieval fortified wall that used to protect the city. Today these boulevards (which are really one continuous street, though the street names keep changing every few blocks), are phenomenally busy, crowded with shops, movies, and cafés. If you have some spare time, you will find it fun to do as the Parisians do. Stroll leisurely on the Grands Boulevards, then sit on the terrace of one of the cafés and watch the cosmopolitan life of the city go by.

L'Opéra. One of the most famous sights of Paris, the Opéra stands in the busiest center of traffic. Its magnificently ornate, Baroque façade dominates the north side of the square. It is lavishly decorated with statues and sculptural groups, including the most famous one of *The Dance* by Carpeaux (next to the last one on the right). Busts of great composers adorn the Italian-style loggia.

If the exterior is imposing, the interior is the acme of luxurious splendor. Its *Grand Staircase* of white marble steps with balustrades made of the finest onyx lead to the even more resplendent *Grand Foyer,* crowded with paintings, sculptures, and dazzling crystal chan-

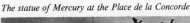
The statue of Mercury at the Place de la Concorde

deliers. During a gala performance the soldiers of the *Garde Républicaine* in fabulous full-dress uniform with shining helmets and drawn sabers stand at attention lining the broad staircase on both sides. With the elegant formal dress of the audience it makes a fairy-tale spectacle. Though in area the Opéra is the largest theater in the world, it seats less than twenty-two hundred people because so much space is taken up by its many lobbies, enormous stage, and grand staircase. The acoustics are not the best, but for splendor of staging and as a sumptuous showplace for the audience, the Opéra is unrivaled.

La Madeleine. The Madeleine is only a short and pleasant walk from the Opéra down the Boulevard des Capucines and the Boulevard de la Madeleine. It is impossible to miss the huge Church of St. Mary Magdalen, styled like a Greek temple, with majestic Corinthian columns on all sides. Though the exterior is striking in its symmetry and grace, the interior is quite conventional. The Madeleine has had a rather stormy history. Originally designed as a church, it was altered to be a "Temple of Glory" in honor of Napoleon's army, then restored as a church, then almost turned into the city's first railway station, and finally consecrated as a church in 1842. Today it has the most fashionable parish in Paris.

As you stand in front of the entrance and look down the long vista of the Rue Royale, past the Place de la Concorde to the Palais Bourbon, a half-mile away on the other side of the Seine, you will be struck by the way the Corinthian façade of the Palais Bourbon exactly complements that of the Madeleine. This harmonious balance becomes even more apparent if you look at both buildings from the Place de la Concorde.

Place de la Concorde. Undoubtedly the most magnificent square in Paris, the Place de la Concorde is considered by many to be the finest in the world. Not so much for the beauty of its buildings—but for the unmatched vistas that open up from this square on every side. The two handsome twin mansions on the north side are the work of Gabriel, the great 18th-century architect. The one on the left is now occupied by the Ministry of Marine, and the one on the right is shared by the luxurious Hotel Crillon, a bank, and the Automobile Club of France. The square is particularly enchanting at night. And on Friday and Saturday, when it is spectacularly flood-lit and the lights play over the waters of the fountains and the 3300-year old Egyptian Obelisk in the center and illuminate the exquisite details of the Gabriel buildings, the place takes on an almost magical quality.

The Place de la Concorde was first designed in 1763 for Louis XV, after whom it was named. Some thirty years later the central statue of the king was hauled down, the name changed to the Place de la Révolution, and Louis XVI's head was chopped off here. During the Reign of Terror it was the bloodiest place in Paris. Besides the king, some three thousand persons were guillotined in its spacious area. After the Revolution the name was changed to Place de la Concorde. When the square was being altered in 1836, King Louis-Philippe, remembering history, cautiously rejected the idea of a royal statue in the center and chose the Luxor Obelisk instead. It is still standing there, and the Place de la Concorde has hardly changed since that time.

FROM THE CONCORDE TO THE ETOILE

Champs-Elysées. The best way to approach the Etoile (officially rebaptized Place Charles de Gaulle, a fact not yet acknowledged in Parisian parlance) is to start from the Place de la Concorde and walk up the Avenue des Champs-Elysées, the finest of all promenades in this city of fine promenades. It stretches for more than a mile, and there are things to see all along the way. Framing the entrance to the Avenue, perched on lofty pedestals, are the two spirited statues of rearing "Numidian Horses Being Tamed by Africans," known as the *Chevaux de Marly.* These were brought here from the Marly Palace near Versailles at the end of the 18th century. The Rond-Point divides the Champs-Elysées into two distinct parts: the eastern half, an immense park with palaces and theaters, and a favorite children's playground with puppet shows and merry-go-rounds. The western part is quite different—a business street flanked by luxurious apartment houses, movies, cafés, and elegant shops. As you walk through the gardens, you will come first upon the palace-like *Théâtre des Ambassadeurs,* followed by the circular *Théâtre de Marigny.* Behind the latter theater is an open-air stamp market, the *Bourse aux Timbres,* a lively place with little tables and chairs, where youngsters and professional collectors gather every Thursday and Sunday.

On the left side of the Champs-Elysées, near the Place Clemenceau, you will see two palaces (the *Petit* is very large and the *Grand* is enormous) that were erected for the Exhibition of 1900 and have been in use ever since. The *Grand Palais* is used for some large exhibitions. One part of it, known as the *Palais de la Découverte* (Palace of Discovery) is a permanent and interesting scientific museum. (See Museum Guide.) The *Petit Palais,* besides being used for various exhibitions, houses the *Beaux-Arts de la Ville de Paris,* the Fine Arts Museum which contains the permanent art collections of the city. It also features French or international art shows that change every few months.

From the Rond-Point to the Etoile, the Champs-Elysées comes alive with fascinating shop windows, fashionable shops, movies, hotels, and large cafés. A popular restaurant and café is *Fouquet's,* a favorite place of established writers, actors, actresses, and directors. That Parisian elegance, which once belonged to the Grands Boulevards, has now touched the Champs-Elysées, too.

Arc de Triomphe. In the midst of the giant rotary at Place de Gaulle rises the glorious heroically scaled Arc de Triomphe, the largest triumphal arch in the world. When Napoleon Bonaparte commissioned the monument in 1806 in honor of the victorious French armies, he stipulated that it be angled in such a way that on his birthday the sun would rise directly over the middle. The Arch is lavishly decorated with enormous sculptures, which look in better proportion when you are not too close. The exception to this is the group by Rude depicting the departure of the Revolutionary army in 1792, usually called *La Marseillaise,* which is definitely a masterpiece. Take the elevator to the top of the Arch. There is a wonderful view of Paris from the platform, and the panoramic pattern formed by the twelve great avenues radiating from Place de Gaulle make it vividly clear why this place is still called *Etoile:* "The Star".

PLACE DU TROCADERO AND VICINITY

Palais de Chaillot. Built as part of the Exhibition of 1937, this palace is a stunning example of modern French architecture. From its vast terrace there is a splendid view of the Eiffel Tower, the Champ de Mars, and the Ecole Militaire on the opposite side of the Seine. The Palais de Chaillot is set in the attractive *Trocadéro Gardens,* whose ornamental lake and many fountains are especially lovely when they are illuminated at night. Another delightful feature of the gardens is the aquarium containing specimens of all the fish found in the rivers of France. Within the palace is the modern *Théâtre du Palais de Chaillot,* and three unusual museums.

Musée National d'Art Moderne. At 11 Avenue du Président-Wilson, quite near the Palais de Chaillot, is the National Museum of Modern Art, devoted to recent and contemporary French painting and sculpture. This collection supplements the work of the Impressionist School in the Jeu de Paume Museum. Among its wealth of fine works by modern artists are paintings by Matisse, Dufy, Bonnard, Vuillard, Utrillo, Rouault, Braque, and Picasso; and sculptures by Maillol, Brancusi, and Bourdelle. The works of art are displayed in an exceptionally fine arrangement, and any one puzzled by the various movements of modern French painting will find illumination in this museum.

Bois de Boulogne. Though its atmosphere is country-like, the Bois de Boulogne (near the Porte Maillot and Porte Dauphine) is very much a

Place de Gaulle from above—the hub of the city

part of Parisian life. Amazingly like a real forest for a place so close to a metropolis, it offers a complete change from the hustle of sight-seeing in the city. The pleasantest way to savor the forest-park is to hire a horse-drawn carriage and just drive around. (Make sure that you find out the price of this luxury before you ride, or else it might come as quite a shock.) Besides its forest area, the Bois has several large lakes with charming islands, a waterfall, and playgrounds. It has many delightful open-air cafés and restaurants, the finest being the de luxe *Pré Catelan,* situated in a lovely garden, and the fashionable *Pavillon d'Armenonville* on the edge of a lake. The famous race tracks of Auteuil and Longchamp are also in the Bois de Boulogne. Near the children's playground is the *Parc de Bagatelle* with a charming little 18th-century palace, which was built on a bet for Charles X in only two months. It is set in a beautiful park, and its brilliant tulip and rose gardens are world famous.

MONTMARTRE

You have a choice of two explanations of how Montmartre got its name. The popular version has it that it was called *Mont des Martyrs* from the three saints who were beheaded there in early Christian times, among them St. Denis, the patron saint of France. Most historians believe that the name originally was *Mont de Mer-cure,* from the temple of Mercury that stood there in Roman times. About 150 years ago Montmartre was an independent little farming village outside of Paris. Vineyards grew on its hillsides, and windmills played in the breeze. Today it is one of the busiest districts of Paris; its population having grown from 2,000 to 240,000. Though commer-cialized, it is still full of picturesque contrasts and surprises.

Montmartre is broken into two distinctly different sections: *Upper Montmartre,* centering around the Place du Tertre, maintains much of the old world atmosphere of the original village; *Lower Mont-martre,* or *Pigalle,* which stretches from the Place Clichy to the Place d'Anvers, is associated with the most scabrous night life in Paris.

Lower Montmartre. If you start at the Place Blanche, you will quickly spot the *Moulin Rouge,* the fabulous dance hall whose fame was made ever more widespread recently by the film of the same name. This was Toulouse-Lautrec's favorite haunt, and his brilliant posters and paintings of the dancing girls and characters who fre-quented it have immortalized the quality of Montmartre life at the turn of the century.

A few blocks east on the Boulevard de Clichy is the *Place Pigalle,* the true center of lower Montmartre and the heart of the entertain-ment district. You will find more night clubs and cabarets here than anywhere else in the world. In the evening when the many elaborate night clubs, informal cabarets, seamy side shows, innumerable movie theaters, and all-night cafés are going in full swing, it is a fantastically hectic place. If you sit outdoors at one of Pigalle's cafés (*not* the best spot to spend an evening in Paris), you may well be approached by a peddler who will try to sell you anything from a carpet to a wallet. A polite "non, merci" will send him away. If you do want to buy something as a souvenir, remember that his asking price is only the beginning, the bargaining is expected.

Upper Montmartre. When you leave Place Pigalle, continue east on the same Boulevard Clichy, though its name now changes to Boulevard Rochechouart, all the way to the Rue Dancourt, which ascends rather steeply on your left. Go up this street and on your right is the charming, small Place Dancourt with the popular *Théâtre de l'Atelier*. Continuing on the Rue des Trois Frères, you will meet the Rue Antoinette about fifty yards further up the hill. This street will bring you to the *Chapelle Auxiliatrice du Purgatoire*, where in 1534 St. Ignatius Loyola and his companions took a vow to found the world-wide Jesuit Order. Continue on this street until it meets the Rue des Abbesses, which in turn runs into the Rue Ravignan. The steep ascent to the top of Montmartre hill, *La Butte*, now begins. Though it may be tiring, going by foot is the best way to get the feel of this unique Parisian community. Walking downhill seems anticlimactic. If you don't feel equal to the climb, you can still see more of the colorful streets than you would if you went by car, by taking the little funicular. To do this, simply continue on the Boulevard Rochechouart until you come to the Rue de Steinkerque. The funicular here will take you right to the top of the hill.

As you ascend the Rue Ravignan, you will soon come across the *Place Emile Goudeau*. Many painters' studios are located in this square, but No. 13, the house where Picasso lived and worked for many years, is no more. As you approach the plateau on top, there is a very noticeable change in the atmosphere. Quite suddenly you are in the old Montmartre; here are the dilapidated, but completely enchanting, houses and the narrow, winding streets of a little village. You have left grandiose Paris far behind.

The *Place du Tertre* has pretty much the same peaceful and country-like atmosphere it had in the 19th century though during the tourist season it gets very crowded. Besides the art galleries and curio shops, there are some excellent outdoor restaurants around here. It is especially pleasant to sip a drink at one of the café tables set out under the trees in the middle of the square.

Before going on to *Sacré Coeur*, whose spiraling white towers peek out from behind the corners of the narrow streets, walk around this old section for a while. It is completely different from the rest of Paris, and even the attitude of its inhabitants is more provincial and more independent. One of the interesting places to visit is the celebrated *chansonnier,* or singing cabaret, known as the *Lapin Agile,* still much the same today as it was in 1900. Its entertainment consists of singing and joking, and if you enter while a show is on, you might well be the target for an improvised satirical song, all in good fun. This used to be the favorite meeting place of Utrillo, Picasso, and many other painters, and it is still frequented by artists and writers.

Take the Rue St. Vincent on the left of the Lapin Agile and turn left again when you get to the Rue Girardon. Near the top of the stairs here you will see two windmills which are part of the dance hall known as *Moulin de la Galette.* This place has been a popular subject for many great artists; Renoir's painting of it in the Jeu de Paume Museum, is the most famous. The Rue Lepic goes past the windmills, and at No. 54 is the house where Vincent Van Gogh lived during his Paris sojourn as an unknown artist. Although Montmartre has changed since those days, it is still very much an important *quartier* for serious, as well as commercial, artists. It is still full of garrets where ambitious young painters work, still full of little islands of non-conformists, and still very much "the free republic of the artists."

Sacré Coeur (Church of the Sacred Heart). Behind the Place du Tertre, crowning the top of Montmartre, rise the strange white Byzantine domes of the basilica of Sacré Coeur. Though it has been even more hotly attacked than the Eiffel Tower as an artistic monstrosity, it would be hard now to imagine Paris without this landmark visible from every part of town. The building of the Sacré Coeur came as a direct result of the French defeat in 1870. Feeling the need for a new symbol of repentance and hope, it was decided to give it expression in a grandiose church. After the National Assembly of 1873 voted to launch a campaign, an enthusiastic public subscribed the tremendous sum of more than forty million francs, and the church was finally dedicated in 1919.

The interior is impressively massive (it can hold some nine thousand people) and has a large mosaic vault and other lavish decora-

Kiosk and Sacré Coeur

tions. Whatever you may think of the inside of the church, which many find showy and mechanical, everyone agrees that the view from the front terrace offers a miraculous panorama of Paris. If you feel energetic enough to climb to the top of the dome, you will have an even better view, including the surrounding countryside for more than thirty miles.

St. Pierre. Just a few yards to the left of Sacré Coeur, as you face it, is a little church, one of the oldest in Paris, dating from the first half of the 12th century. The western façade of St. Pierre was unfortunately rebuilt in the 18th century, and is out of character with the simplicity of the rest of the church. On the other hand, the modern stained-glass windows, done by the artist Max Ingrand in 1953, blend surprisingly well in the original 12th-century apse. Inside are also four interesting columns taken from a Roman temple to Mercury which used to stand on Montmartrè some two thousand years ago.

NEAR THE CITY LIMITS

Marché Aux Puces (The Flea Market). One of the most curious sights of Paris is its world-renowned Flea Market. Situated just outside of the city limits behind the Porte de Clignancourt, and open on Saturday, Sunday, and Monday only, this market sells anything from ancient battle armor and Louis XIV furniture to broken china. The section that sells new goods has nothing of much interest; the visitor should go straight to the fascinating secondhand section. Here the conglomeration of antiques and plain junk is an unbelievable sight, impossible to describe. With a little knowledge of antiques, and a bit of luck, you might find something quite valuable. You are almost certain to find some unusual curiosity and to have the fun of shopping here. Prices may seem high, particularly in the summer tourist months, but remember that haggling is the order of the day here, and the merchant enjoys it as much as the buyer. If you feel shy about bargaining, then you had better stick to small, inexpensive articles.

Parc des Buttes-Chaumont. Generally acclaimed as the most picturesque and one of the most beautiful parks in Paris, the Buttes-Chaumont is the least known because it is situated in a section rarely visited by tourists. This is the large working-class district east of the Place de la République known as *Belleville* and *Menilmontant,* and famous mainly for Maurice Chevalier, who was born here and remembers his old neighborhood fondly in many of his songs. There are no great monuments here, but in its own way this is the most typically French of all the Parisian *quartiers.* The park is built on a high spot with fine views of Paris, and the gardens are informal. An unusual island of rocks, which rises 165 feet right in the middle of the park's lake, is worth seeing. You will find some pleasant cafés and restaurants here, but probably not a single American. It will give you a rounded view of the other side of Paris.

The perfectly preserved Place des Vosges

MUSEUM GUIDE

Paris is blessed with some of the world's most superb museums. The following 22 are suggested as especially rewarding. Unless otherwise noted, these museums are closed on Tuesdays and national holidays, but not on Sundays. Most museums charge an entrance fee of 2–3 francs, half-price (or free) on Sundays.

ART MUSEUMS

Musée des Arts Decoratifs, 107 Rue de Rivoli (1er). 10 A.M. to noon and 2 to 5 P.M. Splendid collection of decorative and ornamental art from medieval to modern times. Closed Mondays and Tuesdays.

Musée de Cluny, 23 Boulevard St. Michel (5e). 9:45 A.M. to 12:45 P.M. and 2 P.M. to 5:15 P.M. Life and art in the Middle Ages, housed in the beautiful Hôtel de Cluny, a medieval French mansion which is in itself a work of art. Closed Tuesdays.

Musée des Gobelins, 42 Avenue des Gobelins (13e). Wed., Thurs., and Fri., 2 to 5 P.M. Unique collection of antique and modern Gobelins tapestry. Don't miss also visiting the workshops where you can see the weavers using their ancient looms.

Musée Guimet, 6 Place d'Iéna (16e). 9:45 A.M. to 12 P.M. and 1:30 P.M. to 5:15 P.M. The religions, history, and arts of the Far East. The Far Eastern collections of the Louvre have recently been transferred here, making it one of the world's finest museums in this field. Closed Tuesdays.

Musée Jacquemart-André, 158 Boulevard Haussmann (8e). Daily, except Mon., 1:30 P.M. to 5:15 P.M. Remarkable collection of French art of the 18th century tastefully arranged in a lovely home. Also some French Renaissance, Italian and Flemish masterpieces.

Musée du Jeu de Paume, end of the Tuileries Gardens at the Place de la Concorde (1er). 9:45 A.M. to 5 P.M. National collection of the Impressionist School of art. Closed Tuesdays.

Pont Neuf

Musée du Louvre, Palais du Louvre (1ᵉʳ). 9:45 A.M. to 5:15 P.M. The largest art museum in the world and perhaps the finest. Sculptures illuminated on Friday night. Closed Tuesdays. Free on Sundays.

Musée National d'Art Moderne, 11 Avenue du Président Wilson (16ᵉ). 9:45 A.M. to 5:15 P.M. Modern art beginning with the Post-Impressionists, brilliantly displayed. Closed Tuesdays. Free on Sundays.

Musée des Monuments Français, in the Palais de Chaillot, Place du Trocadéro (16ᵉ). 9:45 A.M. to 12:30 P.M. and 2 to 5:30 P.M. An ingenious collection of wonderful reproductions of architecture and frescoes. Closed Tuesdays.

Musée Nissim de Camondo, 63 Rue de Monceau (8ᵉ). Daily except Tues. and Wed., 10 A.M. to 12 P.M. and 2 to 5 P.M. Beautiful furniture and art of the 18th century arranged in the fashion of an elegant 18th-century home (closed July).

Musée de l'Orangerie, Place de la Concorde (8ᵉ). 10 A.M. to 5 P.M. Wednesdays open until 10 P.M. Contains permanent Impressionist collection, especially of Monet's greatest work, *Les Nymphéas.* Closed Tuesdays.

Musée Rodin, 77 Rue de Varenne (7ᵉ). 10 A.M. to 12:15 P.M. and 2 to 6 P.M. The works and also the art collections of Auguste Rodin displayed in a handsome mansion. Closed Tuesdays.

HISTORICAL MUSEUMS

Musée de l'Histoire de la France, 60 Rue des Francs-Bourgeois (3ᵉ). 2 to 5 P.M. The history of France illustrated through the outstanding documents of the National Archives, displayed in the beautiful rooms of the 18th-century Hotel Soubise. Closed Tuesdays.

Musée de l'Armée, Hôtel des Invalides (7ᵉ). 10 A.M. to 5 P.M. Largest military museum in the world: arms, armor, and historical souvenirs. Napoleon's tomb is also in the Invalides. Closed Tuesdays.

Musée Carnavalet, 23 Rue de Sévigné (3ᵉ). 10 A.M. to 5:45 P.M. Art, furniture, costumes, and household belongings illustrating the social history of Paris, especially during the Revolution. Closed Mondays and Tuesdays. Free on Sundays.

Musée Victor-Hugo, 6 Place des Vosges (4ᵉ). 10 A.M. to 5:50 P.M. The house where Victor Hugo lived displays a collection of his personal effects, along with drawings and furniture designed by the great French writer. Closed Mondays and Tuesdays, free on Sundays.

Pont Royal

SPECIAL MUSEUMS

Conservatoire des Arts et Metiers, 292 Rue St. Martin (16ᵉ). Daily, except Monday, 1:30 to 5:30; Sunday 10 A.M. to 5 P.M. The patent museum of Paris; remarkable scale model machines.

Musée Grevin, 10 Boulevard Montmartre (9ᵉ). Open weekdays from 2 to 7 P.M., weekends and holidays from 1:30 to 8 P.M. This Paris version of Madame Tussaud's has an entertaining collection of waxworks depicting historical and contemporary famous people.

Musée National d'Histoire Naturelle, in the Jardin des Plantes, 57 Rue Cuvier (5ᵉ). Daily except Tues., 1:30 to 5 P.M. Sundays 10:30 A.M. to 5 P.M. The natural history museum of Paris with unusual exhibits in zoology, mineralogy, and paleontology.

Musée des Arts et Traditions Populaires, Route de Madrid, Bois de Boulogne (Métro: Sablons). 10 A.M. to 12:30 P.M. and 2 to 5 P.M. Lively exhibitions of handicrafts, regional costumes and folklore. Closed Tuesdays.

Musée de l'Homme, in the Palais de Chaillot, Place du Trocadero (16ᵉ). 10 A.M. to 5 P.M. One of the world's most modern and finest anthropological and ethnological displays, showing the civilization of man in all stages. Frequent film showings. Closed Tuesdays.

Palais de la Decouverte, in the Grand Palais, 1 Avenue Franklin Roosevelt (8ᵉ). Daily, except Monday from 10 A.M. to 6 P.M. Fascinating museum of modern discoveries and science, affiliated with the University of Paris. Planetarium performances at 3 and 4:00 P.M., and educational films at 3:30 and 4:30 P.M. on Wednesdays.

Le Panthéon

CHAPTER 5

WHERE TO STAY IN PARIS

Deciding on a hotel in Paris is not at all like deciding where to stay in New York, or San Francisco, or New Orleans, or Washington, D.C. In one way the choice is a good deal simpler—and in another, much harder. It is made simpler by the fantastic profusion of good hotels in Paris. There are elegant hotels, comfortable hotels, modern hotels, and simple hotels in almost every district throughout the city. They are varied enough to suit all tastes and every pocketbook. You need only decide on what suits you best. But there's the difficulty. This same profusion makes the choice a tough one. Do you want the elegance of the Place Vendôme—Opéra area, where within a radius of half a dozen blocks you find three or four of the best-known hotels in the world? Here you can live in ducal splendor at princely prices among the pretenders to half the vacant thrones of Europe. And, in truth, there are also immensely comfortable and reasonably priced hotels here too. Or do you fancy a hotel in the district of the gay and sprightly Champs-Elysées, the greatest great white way in the world? Or would you like to live in the student quarter, or on the river, or high above the town in Montmartre?

If you know Paris, the choice is relatively easy, as you know which one of the many faces of the city suits you best. If you don't, you must decide on the area that promises to appeal to you most and within it choose the hotel whose description and price fulfill your requirements. Unfortunately, it is a choice you must make sight unseen because Paris is the city the world comes to see, and from May to October you must book ahead or be content with second best. Of course, once you are there and have a place to lay your head, you can look around if you aren't happy with your lot. But don't go to Paris with-

re Dame from the Left Bank

out a reservation, or your first days may be spent in a depressing search for a place to stay.

The hotel listing that follows later in the chapter is broken down into six broad areas, each with its own personality. Within the areas the hotels are listed in four categories according to price: de luxe, first class, medium-priced, and inexpensive. The base used for figuring category is the average price of a double room with bath. Other accommodations scale down (or up) from there. Obviously the figures given are not precise but merely indicate range; but they should serve your purposes in deciding at what level you want to spend. Unless prices rise considerably, you may find that in some instances those given here appear a little on the high side—more than the prices quoted by the hotels themselves. Don't be misled. In accordance with European custom Parisian hôteliers add a percentage to all bills, covering taxes and service. It varies from hotel to hotel from a low of about 10 per cent to a high of about 30 per cent, and further it may be included in the price quoted and it may not be. It is really a device to make the costs seem lower and therefore the hotel more inviting, much in the way certain commodities are sold here—i.e., automobiles, the base price for which doesn't include automatic charges like shipping and local taxes. The Europeans are used to it and automatically make the mental addition. It is a system, however, that has made many an American visitor feel he has been taken advantage of—which, of course, is not the case. In any event, the desk clerk is not going to be insulted or shocked if you ask him to give you the room price with service, taxes, and any other automatic extras totalled up—so that you'll know in advance just about what the tab is going to be.

Pensions and Pension Plans. There is no direct American equivalent to the French pension. It is perhaps best described as a cross between a boarding house and an American-plan hotel. At a pension you sign up for board, as well as lodging, and its function is to provide inexpensive accommodations for the visitor who plans to stay for several weeks at least and who wants to avoid the high daily hotel rates. None are given in the listing that follows, but information and advice on pensions in Paris can be had by applying to the Office de Tourisme de Paris, 127 Champs-Elysées.

Pension and demi-pension plans are being required, however, by some hotels. Under the demi-pension arrangement, the management requires that the guest eat breakfast and either lunch or dinner at the hotel. Since this can be extremely limiting to one's activities and since it cuts down the restaurant-testing that every visitor to Paris in possession of his taste buds wants to indulge in, it's a good idea to ascertain before you sign the register whether or not demi-pension is a requirement. Further, since under this system you are charged a flat fee for meals, whether you have a salad or pressed duck, the cost is out of your control, and it may be more than you want to pay.

Tipping. Although the service charges were designed to eliminate tipping, the effort has not been eminently successful. You are still expected to tip the bellboy one franc (more, if you have many heavy bags), the telephone operator if she makes calls for you, and the waiter if he does an extra service. When your bill includes the service charge, you don't have to tip the waiter for bringing your breakfast, the chambermaids or the dining-room waiter. The concierge is a man who should not be forgotten when it comes to tips. He is the one who gets theater tickets for you, calls the restaurant for reservations, gets you a taxi, and so forth. He can do much to make your stay enjoyable. It is the general practice to tip him on checking out of the hotel; some people find it useful to give him half of what they expect to tip at the beginning and the rest at the end. In a medium-priced hotel you might tip the concierge ten new francs for a week's stay plus 15 per cent of his bill if any.

Costs. In comparison with the prices in the provinces and in most other European capitals, lodging in Paris comes dear. But compare it with the prices at home and then take into consideration that in Paris you are living in the most beautiful and exciting city in the world. Some hotels have reduced weekly or monthly rates (ask when you make your reservations). Daily rates for an average double room with bath in the hotels listed here follow:

De Luxe	Over 300 francs	*Over $68*
First Class	200 to 300 francs	*$45 to $68*
Medium-priced	10 to 200 francs	*$23 to $45*
Inexpensive	Under 10 francs	*Under $23*

Except for deluxe hotels, where service charges and taxes amount to about 25% of your bill, prices usually include service and taxes, but not breakfast, which is an extra charge.

OPERA—PLACE VENDOME—PALAIS ROYAL (1er, 2e, 9e)

Here is the heart of Paris for many a visitor. Included in its boundaries are the Louvre and the Opéra, the great shopping streets —Rue de Rivoli, Rue St. Honoré, Rue de la Paix, and the grandest of the grand hotels clustered around Napoleon's column in the Place Vendôme. It is an elegant international section. You will have no difficulty with language here—even the bellboys speak English, or at least understand it, and you will see them studying their Berlitz books while waiting for a call.

A champagne cellar

DE LUXE

Inter-Continental, 3 Rue de Castiglione, 1er. The elegant open court makes a fine meeting place for tea or cocktails. 510 rooms.

Meurice, 228 Rue de Rivoli, 1er. Facing the Tuileries and the river, one of the smartest of Paris' smart hotels. 220 rooms.

Ritz, 15 Place Vendôme, 1er. Often called the best hotel in the world. Certainly the most famous, and justly so. 150 rooms.

Bristol, 112 Rue du Faubourg Saint-Honoré, 8e. Two blocks across the Elysées Palace, a good place for businessmen. 200 rooms.

FIRST CLASS

Ambassador, 16 Blvd. Haussman, 9e. This big, airy, well-kept hotel is a great favorite of both English and American businessmen. 315 rooms.

France-et-Choiseul, 239 Rue St. Honoré, 1er. Beautifully situated and comfortable. Around the corner from the Place Vendôme. 135 rooms.

Grand Hotel, 2 Rue Scribe, 9e. Facing the famous Place de l'Opéra, this enormous hotel runs like clockwork. Convenient. 590 rooms.

Lotti, 7 Rue de Castiglione, 1er. Smaller and a little less expensive than the other grand hotels. An extremely comfortable place to stay. 135 rooms.

Scribe, 1 Rue Scribe, 9e. Down the block from American Express in the same area as the Grand. 200 rooms.

Vendôme, 1 Place Vendôme, 1er. A small but extremely chic neighbor of the Ritz. Nearly all rooms have good views of this fabulous area. 40 rooms.

MEDIUM-PRICED

Louvre, Place du Théâtre-Francais, 1er. At the meeting of the Ave. de l'Opéra, and Rue St. Honoré—a half block from the Louvre. A top-grade hotel with reasonable rates. 240 rooms.

Metropole-Opéra, 2 Rue Gramont, 2e. In the heart of everything. No restaurant. 50 rooms.

Normandy, 7 Rue de l'Echelle, 1er. Toward the top of its price category, this extremely pleasant hotel is within a stone's throw of the Louvre. 140 rooms.

Richmond, 11 Rue du Helder, 9e. One of the better small hotels in the Opéra district. 60 rooms, most with bath.

London Palace, 32 Blvd. des Italiens, 9e. This small hotel has no restaurant, but serves, of course, a regular continental breakfast. 50 rooms.

INEXPENSIVE

Saint-Romain, 7 Rue St. Roch, 1er. On a quiet little street halfway between le Louvre and l'Opéra. 32 rooms.

Favart, 5 Rue Marivaux, 2e. Next door to l'Opéra Comique and halfway between la Comédie Française and l'Opéra—a good place for theater-goers. 40 rooms.

Laffon, 25 Rue Buffault, 9e. Nice little hotel, modest but comfortable. 47 rooms.

CONCORDE—CHAMPS-ELYSEES-TERNES (8e, 17e)

The second major area for the grand hotel is the district dominated by Place de Gaulle and the broad Champs-Elysées. It is *Gay Paree* epitomized. Here is the center of night life—and the kind of sights and sounds that make Paris the home of *Maxim's* and *Fouquet's*. To the north, around the lovely Parc Monceau is one of the city's oldest fashionable residential areas.

DE LUXE

Prince de Galles, 33 Ave. George V, 8ᵉ, near its famous cousin, the George V. 210 rooms.

Crillon, 10 Place de la Concorde, 8ᵉ. Elegant is the word for this old world beauty. The most beautiful situation in Paris. 190 rooms.

George V, 31 Ave. George V, 8ᵉ. The crowd here is glamorous and chic. The haunt of bigwigs in the entertainment world. 215 rooms.

Plaza Athénée, 25 Ave. Montaigne, 8ᵉ. A great hotel with a great restaurant. 213 rooms and 35 salons.

FIRST CLASS

California, 16 Rue de Berri, 8ᵉ. Not far from the Champs-Elysées, an excellent modern hotel. 200 rooms.

Claridge, 74 Ave. Champs-Elysées, 8ᵉ. Almost as elegant as its London namesake. Swimming pool. 300 rooms.

Meridien, 81 Blvd. Gouvion Saint Cyr, 17ᵉ. New, large, comfortable, in the heart of the new commercial district. Restaurants, shops, boutiques. 1033 rooms.

Royal Monceau, 35 Ave. Hoche, 8ᵉ. Halfway between Place de Gaulle and the lovely park from which it takes its name. Very grand in a quiet way. 200 rooms.

MEDIUM-PRICED

Atala, 10 Rue de Chateaubriand, 8ᵉ. A quiet, well-run establishment with all conveniences. A block and a half from the Champs-Elysées. 50 rooms.

Cecilia, 11 Ave. MacMahon, 17ᵉ. Small, in a good residential district north of Place de Gaulle. 44 rooms.

Florida, 12 Blvd. Malesherbes, 8ᵉ. Clean comfortable, near la Madeleine and la Concorde. Restaurant. 47 rooms.

Roblin, 6 Rue Chauveau-Lagarde, 8ᵉ. Near the Madeleine, the Place de la Concorde, and the shops. 70 rooms.

Splendid, 1 bis Ave. Carnot, 17ᵉ. Just to the north of the Arch of Triumph in an open setting. Small and extremely comfortable. 60 rooms.

INEXPENSIVE

Mercédes, 128 Ave. de Wagram, 17ᵉ. Small, friendly and quiet. No restaurant. 35 rooms.

Grand Hôtel de l'Europe, 15 Rue de Constantinople, 8ᵉ. Near the Gare Saint Lazare (Boat trains) and the shopping district. 50 rooms.

Madeleine Plaza, 33 Place de la Madeleine, 8ᵉ. Conveniently located between la Concorde and city's main shopping district.

AVENUE FOCH-PASSY-AUTEUIL (16ᵉ)

If you were to live in Paris, you could find no pleasanter area than this one. Almost without exception residential, it is bounded by the Seine on one side and the Bois de Boulogne on the other.

DE LUXE

Raphael, 17 Ave. Kléber, 16ᵉ. The most luxurious hotel in the area. Lovely terrace garden with view over Paris. 92 rooms.

FIRST CLASS

Iéna, 28 Ave. d'Iéna, 16ᵉ. Justly famous, fairly sizable, well-kept hotel. Across the river from the Eiffel Tower. 108 rooms.

La Pérouse, 40 Rue La Pérouse, 16ᵉ. Up near the Etoile. Its charm is in keeping with its surroundings. 45 rooms.

MEDIUM-PRICED

Massenet, 5 bis Rue Massenet, 16ᵉ. Near the Trocadero Gardens. No restaurant. 43 rooms.

Régina de Passy, 6 Rue de la Tour, 16ᵉ. A block from the river. Pleasant surroundings. 62 rooms.

INEXPENSIVE

Belles Feuilles, 5 Rue des Belles Feuilles, 16ᵉ. Small, comfortable hotel. No restaurant. 30 rooms.

Keppler, 12 Rue Keppler, 16ᵉ. Nice hotel on quiet street near the Etoile. No restaurant. 47 rooms.

INVALIDES-GRENELLE (7ᵉ, 15ᵉ)

Not really a cohesive neighborhood, this area changes face as you move through it. Down by the river on the Quai d'Orsay and toward the Eiffel Tower are big apartment houses and the open spaces of the Invalides esplanade and the Champ de Mars. Out to the south is the great middle-class residential area of the 15th arrondissement, stretching toward the suburbs. In the east begins the Paris of Hemingway and Gertrude Stein, the *Left Bank*.

DE LUXE

Paris Hilton, 18 Ave. de Suffren, 15ᵉ. In the Hilton tradition. The Restaurant at the top, *Le Toit de Paris*, has one of the best views of the city. 492 rooms.

Sofitel Bourbon, 32 Rue St. Dominique, 7ᵉ. Brand new and elegant, on the left bank. 115 rooms.

FIRST CLASS

Montalembert, 3 Rue Montalembert, 7ᵉ. Next door to the grander Pont Royal. A favorite with many. 63 rooms.

Pont Royal, 7 Rue Montalembert, 7ᵉ. An excellent Left Bank hotel. One of the plushest on this side of the river. Excellent restaurant. 80 rooms.

MEDIUM-PRICED

Cayré, 4 Blvd. Raspail, 7ᵉ. Just off the fabulous Blvd. St. Germain. 140 rooms.

Quai Voltaire, 19 Quai Voltaire, 7ᵉ. Superbly located on the Seine. No restaurant. 32 rooms.

Saxe Residence, 9 Villa de Saxe, 7ᵉ. A quiet place in a residential area. No restaurant. 53 rooms.

Derby, 5 Ave. Duquesne, 7ᵉ. Behind the Invalides and across the street from the Ecole Militaire. 43 rooms.

INEXPENSIVE

Vaneau, 85 Rue Vaneau, 7ᵉ. No restaurant. 52 rooms.

Résidence du Champs de Mars, 19 Rue du Champs de Mars, 7ᵉ. Small, comfortable hotel a stone's throw from the Eiffel Tower and surrounding gardens. 37 rooms.

QUARTIER LATIN—MONTPARNASSE (5ᵉ, 6ᵉ, 13ᵉ, 14ᵉ)

Just as Place Vendôme is the center of Paris for the *haut monde,* the heartbeat of the city's intellectuals is here on the Left Bank in the districts of the Latin Quarter and Montparnasse. Four broad boulevards are the key to this world of artists and students—St. Germain and Montparnasse, St. Michel and Raspail. This is the informal Paris—where the street cafés are filled with beards and serious talk and gaiety. The hotels and restaurants here are less formal too.

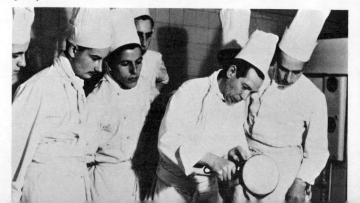

FIRST CLASS

Lutetia, 43 Blvd. Raspail, 6ᵉ. Very large. Not far from the Luxembourg Gardens. 306 rooms.

Relais Bisson, 37 Quai des Grands Augustins, 6ᵉ. Well known mainly for having one of the best restaurants in Paris. Beautiful setting on the river. 30 rooms.

P.L.M. St. Jacques, 17 Blvd. St. Jacques, 14ᵉ. Luxurious modern hotel near Montparnasse. Several restaurants and shopping center in building. 492 rooms.

MEDIUM-PRICED

L'Aiglon, 232 Blvd. Raspail, 14ᵉ. A good hotel in the artists' quarter. No restaurant. 54 rooms.

Madison, 143 Blvd. Saint Germain, 6ᵉ. Smallish and comfortable. A stone's throw from the Café Flore and the Deux Magots. 62 rooms.

Saints Pères, 65 Rue des Saints Pères, 6ᵉ. A favorite of many old Paris hands. Recently renovated. Reserve early. 59 rooms.

St. Simon, 14 Rue St. Simon, 7ᵉ. Quaint little hotel with lovely garden-courtyard located on quiet street. 34 rooms.

INEXPENSIVE

Seine, 52 Rue de Seine, 6ᵉ. Nice, small hotel in the heart of Left Bank art district. 30 rooms.

Saint Sulpice, 7 Rue Casimir Delavigne, 6ᵉ. No restaurant. 43 rooms.

Hotel des Grandes Ecoles, 75 Rue du Cardinal Lemoine, 5ᵉ. At the top of la Montagne Sainte Geneviève, a quiet place overlooking a lovely garden. 30 rooms.

HOTEL DE VILLE—GARE DE LYON (3ᵉ, 4ᵉ, 11ᵉ, 12ᵉ)

If you want to see a part of Paris where the tourist is a rarity, go east, across the Blvd. de Sébastopol. This is a hard-working section of Paris—without frou-frou and without pretension. The Place de la Bastille is here; so is the lovely Place des Vosges; so is the Memorial to the Unknown Jewish Martyrs. But sight-seeing in the conventional sense is not the drawing card here. Here is where you go to get to know the working Frenchman—and who knows, it may be an experience that will last a lifetime. There are not many hotels in this area with the creature comforts expected by most travelers. Two of them, both in the Inexpensive category are: **Moderne Palace,** 3 bis Place de la République, 11ᵉ, and **Modern Hotel Lyon,** 3 Rue Parrot, 12ᵉ, on a quiet street close to the Gare de Lyon.

GARE DU NORD—MONTMARTRE (10ᵉ, 18ᵉ)

Montmartre, the *quartier* on top of Paris' highest hill, still calls itself a village, and in a way it still has some of that character. The old artists' quarter, with its picturesque Place du Tertre is probably the most painted spot in Paris.

FIRST CLASS

Terrasse, 12 Rue Joseph de Maistre, 18ᵉ. The best and biggest hotel in the area. 110 rooms.

Pavillon, 36 Rue de l'Echiquier, 10ᵉ. In a residential district. 214 rooms.

MEDIUM-PRICED

Blanche Fontaine, 34 Rue Fontaine, 9ᵉ. Near Pigalle at the bottom of the Butte Montmartre. 41 rooms.

Terminus Est, 5 Rue 8 Mai 1945, 10ᵉ. Near the Place de la République, in a commercial district. 200 rooms.

INEXPENSIVE

Alsina, 39 Avenue Junot, 18ᵉ. In the heart of the district. 45 rooms.

Hotel Paradis, 11 Place Emile Goudeau, 18ᵉ. A quiet, charming little place, almost on top of the Butte. 40 rooms.

CHAPTER 6

Dining in Paris—anywhere in France, in fact, but especially in Paris—is unlike dining anywhere else, for a number of reasons that will become clear to you the first time you enter a restaurant. There are three principal factors: 1) The food is better; 2) The service is better; 3) it takes longer. The first two points are self-explanatory; the third is less obvious. Generally, food is prepared only to order—and that, of course, takes time. The French don't object to that; they take pride in their food and they enjoy taking time to savor it. For the Parisian, a two-hour lunch period is not unusual. And unlike the Spaniard, he doesn't go to sleep; he eats.

There is no need to extol the virtues of Parisian food. For generations the city has been the Mecca of all gastronomes. And so it is still. It takes a disputatious man to deny that Paris has more restaurants, greater restaurants, and finer food than any other city in the world.

But don't make the mistake of thinking that the food of Paris is all *haute cuisine*. The restaurants—and there are thousands of them—serve an infinite variety of foods ranging all the way from the exquisite gastronomical creations of master chefs to the traditional fare of the provinces. Whatever there is in food can be found in Paris. Your problem is as simple as it is vast. You merely have to find the kind of restaurant and the kind of food you want.

This guide obviously cannot describe or even list more than a fraction of the restaurants in Paris. But it does cover a very wide range from the most famous to the modest places where the food and atmosphere are both good—and made all the more interesting and palatable by being inexpensive.

Alexandre Dumaine, one of France's most famous chefs

In the listing that follows you will find exactly eighty restaurants; more than enough, surely, to appease your appetite during a leisurely visit to Paris. For convenience they have been grouped by area using the same geographical set-up as in the chapter on hotels. Within each group the restaurants are further divided roughly on the basis of price. No one, of course, can tell you just how much you are going to spend for a meal, for food is a matter of personal taste and preference. You will, however, find the classification used here more than a little helpful. Remember that many, many restaurants close during the month of August, and shut down one day a week all year. Don't forget to phone for reservations.

You'll have to pay 5F to 12F for a scotch and 5F up for brandy. Here is what you can expect to pay for dinner for two at the restaurants listed:

Ultra De Luxe	160F to 355F	*$38 to $84*
De Luxe	110F to 200F	*$26 to $47*
Medium-Priced	80F to 140F	*$19 to $33*
Inexpensive	Under 80F	*$19*

For many visitors the scores and hundreds of good *Inexpensive* restaurants in Paris are one of its great delights. It has been said that it is impossible to get a bad meal in Paris, a doubtful assertion, at best. But certainly it is very easy to get a good one, and to get it for a very low price—sometimes substantially under $19.

The *Medium-Priced* restaurants offer excellent food, and service to match. *De Luxe* means superior food and the finest service—and remember that wine and service charge are extra. It's quite possible to spend a good deal more than $47 if you're in the Midas mood.

Finally, in Paris there are a few superb restaurants that rank among the world's finest—according to many, absolutely the greatest. At these *Ultra De Luxe temples of gastronomy,* it's not difficult to spend over $84 with wine, brandy and cigars (plus service charge). But your meal will be worth every penny. You will find these at the head of our list, which by common consent is where they belong.

THE TEMPLES OF GASTRONOMY

Le Grand Vefour, 17 Rue Beaujolais, 1er. The patrons are distinguished, the setting 18th century, the wine list comprehensive, and the food represents the best in the great tradition of French cuisine. In short, there is no better food than this.

Taillevent, 15 Rue Lamennais, 8e. One of the most charming and pleasant restaurants in the city. This is the place to sample non-Parisian French cuisine, for the kitchen specializes not in the manner of one province but in the most notable dishes of them all. And the wine list is even more complete than the menu.

Fabulous food and glamorous surroundings have made the Tour d'Argent the world's most famous restaurant

Maxim's, 3 Rue Royale, 8ᵉ. Even before it was used as the setting for "The Merry Widow" this was one of Paris' favorites. There was a special table for Edward VII, more recently occupied by Princess Margaret, and the best known faces in the world add their glamor to the glitter of this jovially elegant establishment.

Lasserre, 17 Ave. F.D. Roosevelt, 8ᵉ. Open-air dining in the summer, chic and delicious any time of year.

Le Vivarois, 192 Ave. Victor Hugo, 16ᵉ. Brand new addition to the prestigious Michelin three-star rank. The promotion is well-deserved; their "roasted" lobster and everything else is top-notch.

Tour d'Argent, 15 Quai Tournelle, 5ᵉ. A landmark in Paris. A superb view of Notre Dame, magnificent food—a once (at least) in a lifetime experience. Pressed duck is the specialty.

Among other gastronomic temples notable equally for their romantic settings and exquisite fare are: **Franc Pinot,** 1 Quai de Bourbon on the Ile Saint Louis; **Mouton de Panurge,** 17 Rue de Choiseul and the **Restaurant de la Tour Eiffel.**

OPERA—PLACE VENDOME—PALAIS ROYAL (1ᵉʳ, 2ᵉ, 9ᵉ)

DE LUXE

Auberge du Vert Galant, 42 Quai des Orfèvres, 1ᵉʳ. Charming setting beside the river with summer sidewalk terrace. One of Paris' better restaurants.

Café de la Paix, 12 Blvd. Capucines, 9ᵉ. This is *the* café—sidewalk, that is—for meals, for snacks, but most especially for sitting, sipping, and watching Paris along the boulevard. Indoors: snacks to deluxe dinners.

Drouant, Place Gaillon, 2ᵉ. Pleasant and convenient, surrounded by fine hotels and near the Opera.

Escargot Montorgueil, 38 Rue Montorgueil, 1er. Decorated in silver and dark wood. The specialties: seafood and, of course, snails (escargots).

MEDIUM-PRICED

Delmonico, 39 Ave. de l'Opéra.
La Cloche D'Or, 3 Rue Mansart, 9e. Very good food. Open till 6 A.M.
La Galiote, 6 Rue Gomboust.
Pharamond, 24 Rue Grande Truanderie, 1er. Famous, on a side street near the markets. Good food and atmosphere from 7 A.M.

A La Bonne Fourchette, 320 Rue St. Honore. 1e. Delightful Belgian cuisine.
Aux Lyonnais, 32 Rue St. Marc, 2e. Specialties from the most famous gastronomical city in France.

INEXPENSIVE

Ancien Gauclair, 96 Rue Richelieu, 2e.
Le Sherwood, 3 Rue Daunou, 2e. A menu of 112 sorts of dishes in a fun place. Open till 6 A.M.
Poccardi, 9 Blvd. des Italiens, 2e. Italian. Large and cheerful.

CONCORDE—CHAMPS-ELYSEES-TERNES (8e, 17e)

DE LUXE

Ledoyen, carré Champs-Elysées, 8e. One of the few restaurants of Paris indisputably in the grand style. (Closed Sunday, and August.)
Crillon, 10 Place de la Concorde, 8e. Tasteful, subtle elegance—a bit of another, quieter age away from the rush of the boulevards.
Joseph, 56 Rue Pierre-Charron, 8e. Long a favorite with Parisiens, but not so well-known to tourists. Elegant, small.
The Ritz, 15 Place Vendôme, 1er. There can be few hotel dining rooms better than this one. Hemingway and Scott Fitzgerald are but two of the novelists whose characters have frequented the fabulous Ritz bars, where they serve the best martini in Paris. The cuisine is equally—and rightfully—famous.

Plaza Athénée, 25 Ave. Montaigne, 8e. A great hotel restaurant (as good as the Ritz, but cheaper). In summer, dining on the courtyard terrace.

MEDIUM-PRICED

Alexandre, 53 Ave. George V, 8e.
Chez André, 12 Rue Marbeuf, 8e. Typical French bistrot a step from the Champs-Elysées.
Le Righi, 11 Rue La Tremoille, 8e. Top-notch Italian food.
Androuët, 41 Rue d'Amsterdam, 9e. Specializes in cheeses—the most extraordinary assortment you can find in France.
Brasserie Lorraine, 2 Place Ternes 8e. Good eastern French food, reasonable.

The Bois de Boulogne, site of several elegant restaurants

There are lovely walks everywhere in the city

Chez Francis, 7 Place d'Alma, 8ᵉ. Flower-lined terrace and good cuisine.

INEXPENSIVE

Corsaire Basque, 15 Rue Arc De Triomphe, 17ᵉ. Basque dishes—especially the hardy cassoulets flavored with wine and herbs—are delicious, and delightfully different from Parisian cuisine.

Chez Edgard, 4 Rue Marbeuf, 8ᵉ. The place has been remodelled, the patrons are new, and it's still good for lunch or dinner. Open till 1 A.M.

La Marotte, 4 Rue de Parme, 9ᵉ. The patrons are British, but the food is very French. Open daily, except Sunday, until 2:00 A.M.

AVENUE FOCH-PASSY-AUTEUIL (16ᵉ)

DE LUXE

Petit Bedon, 38 Rue Pergolèse, 16ᵉ. There isn't a place more elegant—in decor, in cuisine, or in clientele.

Prunier Traktir, 16 Ave. Victor Hugo, 16ᵉ. Enticing and imaginative cooking.

Pavillon Royal, Bois de Boulogne, 16ᵉ. Open only in spring and summer when the trees and flowers of the Bois are at their loveliest.

Pré Catelan, Bois de Boulogne, 16ᵉ. One of Paris' gayest, and best-known De Luxe restaurants.

MEDIUM-PRICED

San Francisco, 1 Rue Mirabeau, 16ᵉ. There's more of Rome than the Golden Gate here; the Italian food is superb.

Le George Sand, 59 Rue La Fontaine, 16ᵉ. Everything is well-prepared; but the crêpes George Sand are extraordinary.

INEXPENSIVE

Cyprien, 75 Ave. Kleber, 16ᵉ.

Le Relais, 135 Rue Michel Ange, 16ᵉ. Closed Sundays and holidays.

INVALIDES-GRENELLE (7ᵉ, 15ᵉ)

DE LUXE

Tour Eiffel, Champs de Mars, 7ᵉ. Two restaurants—one on the first and one on the second level serve you fine meals and the greatest view Paris has to offer. (Lunch only from Nov. to April.)

La Bourgogne, 6 Ave. Bosquet, 7ᵉ. Small and charming. A fine place to dine, with a sidewalk café atmosphere.

Le Bistrot de Paris, 33 Rue de Lille, 7ᵉ. Closed Saturday and Sunday.

MEDIUM-PRICED

Galant Verre, 12 Rue de Verneuil, 7ᵉ. Fashionable small restaurant with fine food. Reserve several days ahead.

Antoine et Antoinette, 16 Ave. Rapp, 7ᵉ. Good food in a typically Parisian setting.

QUARTIER LATIN—MONTPARNASSE (5ᵉ, 6ᵉ, 13ᵉ, 14ᵉ)

DE LUXE

Lapérouse, 51 Quai Grands Augustins, 6ᵉ. A series of small, old-fashioned rooms make up this restaurant whose reputation for superb cuisine has been maintained for generations. Chicken, and souffles which cover the plate are the specialties.

Relais Louis XIII, 8 Rue Grands-Augustins, 6ᵉ. Great eating in an atmosphere of old Paris.

Meditérranee, 2 Place de l'Odéon, 6ᵉ. Some say it's the best place in Paris for seafood.

Les Marronniers, 53 bis Blvd. Arago, 13ᵉ. Out near the Porte d'Italie, and the splendid food makes the trip worthwhile—or stop on your way to Orly.

MEDIUM-PRICED

A la Grenouille, 26 Rue Grands Augustins, 6ᵉ. Left Bank, lively and a little lewd.

Chez Marius, 30 Rue Fosses St. Bernard, 5ᵉ. Small and simple with

INEXPENSIVE

Des Ministères, 30 Rue du Bac, 7ᵉ.

Au Beaujolais, 17 Rue de Lourmel, 15ᵉ. One of the last authentic bistrots of Paris, the food is very simple, good, cheap. Closed Sundays and August.

Relais de Sèvres, 64 Rue Sèvres, 7ᵉ.

Left Bank atmosphere and the best of food.

Chez Lipp, 151 Blvd. St. Germain, 6ᵉ. Sartre used to be a regular, one of Paris' oldest brasseries. Open till 1 A.M. Closed Mondays and July.

Cochon de Lait, 7 Rue Corneille, 6ᵉ. Charming atmosphere, good food.

Dominique, 19 Rue Brea, 6ᵉ. Not for Ritz habitués, but one of the most authentic Russian places in Paris.

La Coupole, 102 Blvd. du Montparnasse, 14ᵉ. A popular rendezvous for artists and jet setters. Big, garish and noisy, art nouveau décor.

INEXPENSIVE

Vagenende, 142 Blvd. St. Germain, 6ᵉ. Lively, turn-of-the-century atmosphere.

Pizzeria Positano, 15 Rue des Canettes, 6ᵉ. One of the best pizzerias on the Left Bank.

La Talmouze, 1 Rue Laplace, 5ᵉ. Lovely setting. Dinner only.

Paris has a restaurant to serve every taste

Place du Tertre—Montmartre

HOTEL DE VILLE—GARE DE LYON (3ᵉ, 4ᵉ, 11ᵉ, 12ᵉ)

DE LUXE

Coconnas, 2 bis Place des Vosges, 4ᵉ. Old-world charm on one of the loveliest ancient squares in Paris.

MEDIUM-PRICED

Hostellerie Nicolas Flamel, 51 Rue Montmorency, 3ᵉ. An old inn—in fact, an historic monument dating back to 1407. The cuisine is up-to-date and good.

Brasserie Bofinger, 5 Rue de la Bastille, 4ᵉ. Gay and very "in" at the moment. Good food.

INEXPENSIVE

Au Gourmet de l'Isle, 42 Rue St. Louis en l'Ile, 4ᵉ. An old inn on the Ile St. Louis. Provincial specialties.

La Boule d'Or, 15 Place d'Aligre, 12ᵉ. Just off a market square. Another out of the way, locally popular place where tourists are the exception.

GARE DU NORD—MONTMARTRE (10ᵉ, 18ᵉ, 19ᵉ)

DE LUXE

Cochon d'Or, 192 Ave. Jean Jaures, 19ᵉ. Off the beaten track, in the slaughter-house area. Prime meats, superbly grilled.

Chez Michel, 10 Rue Belzunce, 10ᵉ. Excellent cuisine, reserve early.

MEDIUM-PRICED

Au Boeuf Couronné, 188 Ave. Jean Jaures, 19ᵉ. The best *côte de boeuf* in Paris. Near La Villette.

Au Chateaubriant, 23 Rue Chabrol, 10ᵉ. Unpretentious in appearance, but the Italian food is impressive enough to need no decoration.

Relais Paris-Est, Gare de L'Est, second floor. A convenient and very good restaurant.

Mère Catherine, 6 Place du Tertre, 18ᵉ. Montmartre—charming and old. Outside tables in summer.

INEXPENSIVE

Le Relais de la Butte, 12 Rue Ravignan, 18ᵉ. Unusual and delicious special dishes at reasonable prices.

Cochor Lagué, 8 Rue Eugène Sue, 18ᵉ. Reasonable and good. Dinner only.

Les Bosquets, 39 Rue d'Orsel, 18ᵉ. A good address for big eaters. Lovely summer garden.

CHAPTER 7

Paris is the world center of feminine high fashion. Though the *haute couture* of the big fashion designers is beyond the reach of most women, the best buy is still anything that has to do with fashion (except summer sport clothes and shoes)—blouses, lingerie, hats, fabrics, knitted sweaters and dresses, handbags, umbrellas, scarves, and other accessories. Other good buys are the luxury articles for which Paris is noted—perfumes, liqueurs, ceramics, French dolls, art, and antiques.

Gift Buying. Some stores specialize in tourist export, and exhibit a wide variety of products. They will pack, crate, and deliver purchases to your boat or plane, and may offer discounts if you pay in travelers' checks. The largest are:

> *Raoul et Curly*, 47 Ave. de l'Opéra.
> *Helene Dale*, 7 Rue Scribe.
> *Obéron*, 9 Rue Scribe.
> *Paris Opéra*, 43 Rue St. Augustin and (new) 18 Ave. de l'Opéra.
> *Swelly*, 17 Place Vendôme.
> *Parfumerie des Pyramides*, 4 Place des Pyramides.
> *Michel Swiss*, 16 Rue de la Paix.

Two other popular places for picking up characteristically Parisian items for the folks back home are the *bouquinistes* and the *Flea Market*. The former are the little stalls along the banks of the Seine where you can buy interesting old books, old maps, coins, medals, prints, and other Parisian sundries that make welcome gifts. The Flea Market, near the Porte de Clignancourt (see the chapter on WHAT TO SEE), sells just about anything and everything, and it's easy to find some really unique gift.

Department Stores. If you are at a loss for ideas about what to bring back, browsing through one of the main department stores will give you a good over-all picture of what's available in Paris. (See chapter on THINGS TO KNOW for hours.)

> *Au Printemps,* 64 Boulevard Haussmann.
> *Galeries Lafayette,* 40 Boulevard Haussmann.
> *Aux Trois Quartiers,* 17 Boulevard de la Madeleine.
> *Samaritaine,* 75 Rue de Rivoli.
> *Samaritaine de Luxe,* 27 Boulevard des Capucines.
> *Franck et Fils,* 80 Rue de Passy.
> *La Belle Jardiniére,* 2 Rue du Pont-Neuf.
> *Au Bon Marché,* 135 Rue du Bac (on the Left Bank.)

The really exciting shopping is not in the department stores, of course, but in the wonderful specialty shops for which Paris is world famous. It's here that you find the ultimate in taste and quality and that individual touch of imagination that spells "Made in France." Even window dressing is a high art in these places; one that has made window shopping a Parisian passion and a tourist's delight. Though the shops are alphabetically arranged here under the categories of their specialty, bear in mind that those which sell handbags, for example, usually also stock umbrellas, belts, and other leather items; that handkerchiefs and silk scarves—those ideal flat gifts—can be found in all shops that sell any fashion accessories. The places listed here are not cheap (Paris is not for bargain shopping), but they are all well established, with superior merchandise that is well worth the price.

Bookstalls along the Seine on the Left Bank

The critics: at the Ecole des Beaux Arts and on the Pont des Arts

Antiques. The favorite hunting ground for antiques are the innumerable small shops on the Left Bank, especially in the small area extending from the banks of the Seine to the Boulevard St. Germain, between the Rue des Saints Pères and Rue Danton. The Rue Bonaparte is particularly rich in such shops. Though prices seem to rise during the busy tourist months, you can still find good buys here. If you purchase anything more than 100 years old, ask the dealer for a certificate to avoid paying duty on it. Another favorite place is the section of the enormous Flea Market known as Marché Biron, where more than 200 open-air antique stalls are bunched together. This list of some of the most prominent dealers may help to orient you in the vast and perhaps bewildering world of French antiques.

RIGHT BANK

Kraemer, 43 Rue de Monceau.

Mavon, 238 Rue du Faubourg St. Honoré.

Cailleux, 136 Faubourg St. Honoré.

Chalom, 17 Place Vendôme. Also basement bargain boutique.

Doucet, 94 Rue du Faubourg St. Honoré.

La Cour Aux Antiquaires, 54 Rue du Faubourg St. Honoré.

Jansen, 9 Rue Royale.

A Colin Maillard, 11 Rue de Miromesnil.

LEFT BANK

Grognot, 1 Rue des Saints-Pères.

Ronia, 11 Rue des Saints-Pères.

Village Suisse, Ave. La Motte Picquet-Ave. de Suffren. Collection of antiquaries and second-hand dealers.

Art Galleries (Commercial). For centuries Paris has been the city to which young artists from all over the world have come to live and work, and innumerable art shows and galleries crowd the city with their work. Those that are the most fun to browse through are the small galleries that show unknown or relatively obscure painters. Those on the Left Bank are located mainly on the side streets of Montparnasse and St. Germain-des-Prés. When you visit them, remember that it was in just such places that only twenty-five years ago, a young artist named Bernard Buffet was selling his paintings for 50 to 100 dollars. Today, these canvasses are worth a hundred times as much. Happy hunting!

Blouses. The exquisite handmade blouses of Paris are unrivaled. Found in the specialty shops, they also abound in the shops along the Rue du Faubourg St. Honoré.

> *Candide,* 4 Rue de Miromesnil.
> *Mony,* 33 Avenue de l'Opéra. Also large stock of lingerie and made-to-measure dresses.
> *Jane Parent,* 50 Rue du Colisée.
> *Jeanne Pradels,* 1 Rue de la Pépinière.
> *Grande Maison de Blanc*, inside *Drugstore Opéra*, 8 Place de l'Opéra.

Books. Bookstores are all over Paris, but the pleasantest way to shop for books is in the picturesque bookstalls along the quays of the Seine. The following large bookstores specialize in English books, as well as French, and stock magazines, stationery, games, and picture cards.

> *Brentano's,* 37 Avenue de l'Opéra. Good selection of American books.
> *Galignani's,* 224 Rue de Rivoli. Specializes in art books.
> *W. H. Smith & Sons,* 248 Rue de Rivoli. Also has excellent tearoom.
> *Nouveau Quartier Latin,* 78 Blvd. St. Michel. American paperbacks and textbooks.

Ceramics and Crystal. The Paris stores stock all the ware for which France is celebrated, from the rustic pottery of the Riviera villages and the famous Quimper ware of Brittany, to the modern abstract designs of Picasso.

> *Au Vase Etrusque,* 11 Place de la Madeleine. Classic porcelain and crystal, Sèvres and Royal Copenhagen ware.
> *Baccarat,* 30 bis Rue de Paradis. The most exquisite crystal.
> *Delvaux,* 18 Rue Royale. Wide selection at moderate prices of glass, china, and exclusive table decorations.
> *Lalique,* 11 Rue Royale. The finest crystal and china.
> *Limoges Unic,* 12 Rue de Paradis. Really good buys.

Boat Pond in the Luxembourg Gardens

Children's Clothing and Toys. French clothes for children are amazingly smart and beautifully made; any girl would be delighted with a Paris frock. *Au Printemps, Galeries Lafayette, Grande Maison de Blanc* and *Aux Trois Quartiers* have fine selections, less expensive than the specialty shops. French dolls, too, make delightful gifts.

> *A l'Enfant Cheri,* 36 Rue La Boétie.
>
> *Agnes,* 59 Ave. Kleber.
>
> *Au Nain Bleu,* 408 Rue St. Honoré, is a wonderful toy store. Largest and best stock in Paris.
>
> *Helen Vanner,* 402 Rue St. Honoré. One of the best for beautiful (and expensive) girls' clothes.

Parfum?

Clothes For Women. An *haute couture* show is one of the most impressive of Parisian arts. Unless you are a regular customer or buyer, it is almost impossible to get in to see the big Spring and Fall showings. At other times you can see the collection if you obtain an invitation. To do so telephone to the house in advance, telling the day you wish to come; if you have no introduction, you may need your passport for identification. If you are staying at a first-class hotel, your concierge will be able to make the arrangements for you. The house will assign you a saleswoman to answer your questions, but there will not be the slightest pressure on you to buy. Prices at the big-name designers are, of course, astronomically high. Many of the leading designers, however, also have boutiques where ready-to-wear garments (carrying the famous name on the label) are much less. In this list of

If it isn't for sale at the Flea Market, it doesn't exist

well-known houses, those preceded by a (B) have boutiques that sell
ready-to-wear clothes, as well as the usual accessories.

(B) *Vicky Tiel*, 21 Rue Bonaparte (633 38–80).

(B) *Balmain*, 44 Rue François Ier (225 68–04).

(B) *Pierre Cardin*, 118 Faubourg St. Honoré (225 06-23).

(B) *Carven*, 6 Rond-Point des Champs-Elysées (225 66-50).

(B) *Chanel*, 31 Rue Cambon (073 60-21).

(B) *Christian Dior*, 30 Avenue Montaigne (359 93–64).

(B) *Courrèges*, 40 Rue François Ier (359 72–17).

(B) *Givenchy*, 3 Ave. George V (225 92–60).

    Gres, 1 Rue de la Paix (073 01–15).

    Molyneux, 5 Rue Royale (265 68–40).

(B) *Ted Lapidus*, 37 Ave. Pierre Ier de Serbie (225 52–44).

(B) *Lanvin*, 22 Rue du Faubourg St. Honoré (265 27–21).

(B) *Guy Laroche*, 29 Ave. Montaigne (225 57–66).

(B) *Jean Patou*, 7 Rue St. Florentin (073 08–71).

(B) *Madeleine de Rauch*, 37 Avenue Jean-Goujon (359 26–26).

(B) *Philippe Venet*, 32 Ave. George V (256 24–06).

(B) *Yves St. Laurent*, 30 bis Rue Spontini (727 43–79).

(B) *Jean Louis Scherrer*, 51 Ave. Matignon (359 55–39).

Fabrics. French fabrics are not cheap, but they are beautiful and of the highest quality. Beside the department stores, a good place to look for them is on the Rue St. Florentin and Rue Boissy d'Anglas.

> *Bouchara*, 54 Blvd. Haussmann. One of the best for its wide selection of all kinds of fabrics. Branches in other parts of town.
> *Dreyfus,* 1 Place St. Pierre (lower Montmartre). Sells bargain remnants from the big designer houses.
> *Wilmart,* 25 Place Vendôme. Beautiful and expensive fabrics.

Gloves. Fine glove-making is one of the national industries of France. The beautiful gloves are excellent buys and make perfect gifts. They can be bought all over Paris, but the following shops specialize in top quality and design.

> *Robera*, 71 Rue la Boétie.
> *Schilz*, 30 Rue Caumartin.
> *Nicolet,* 18 Rue Duphot. Gloves for children, too.
> *Perrin,* 45 Avenue de l'Opéra and 22 Rue Royale.

Handbags. The custom-made handbags of Paris are expensive, but the last word in beauty and fine craftmanship. If you don't find what you want in the specialty shops listed here, you will surely find it in the many elegant shops of the Rue Cambon, the Rue du Faubourg St. Honoré, the couturier boutiques, or in department stores, where handbags are lower-priced but good.

> *Lancel*, 9 Place de l'Opéra. High class leather goods including superb luggage.
> *Germaine Guerin,* 243 Rue St. Honoré. Noted for exquisite custom-made evening bags.
> *Hermès,* 24 Rue Faubourg St. Honoré. Magnificent and expensive handbags. Also their famous silk scarves and gloves.
> *Léo Miller,* 12 Rue de Castiglione. Large selection of exclusive designs, reasonably priced for high quality.

Paris is a Sunday painter's dream

Hats. Many women who do not dream of custom-made clothes from the couturiers can indulge in a chapeau from one of the leading modistes. There are also hundreds of talented inexpensive milliners throughout Paris who will quickly alter to your taste any hat that catches your eye in their window. If you are buying one for a gift, choose from the adaptable cocktail hats, made out of veiling and ribbons or the artificial flowers for which Paris is famous.

If the two below seem too *grande,* check the department stores and the boutiques.

> *Motsch*, 42 Ave. George V.
> *Paulette*, 63 Avenue Franklin D. Roosevelt.

Jewelry (costume). Paris is noted for its beautifully designed jewelry, whether fake or real. The couturier boutiques sell smart costume jewelry, and you find tempting collections all along the Rue de la Paix, Rue du Faubourg St. Honoré, and in the small shops of the Left Bank.

> *Bijou Burma,* 16 Rue de la Paix, 8 Boulevard des Capucines, and 63 Avenue des Champs-Elysées. Jewelry that looks amazingly real.
> *Casty,* 3 Rue de Castiglione.
> *Line Vautrin,* 29 Quai Grands-Augustins. Tops in fine designs.
> *Técla,* 2 Rue de la Paix. Specializes in pearls.
> *Fabrice,* 26 Rue Bonaparte.

Linens (household). The famed handmade and hand-embroidered linens of France are worth bringing home and make elegant and no-

The Paris street markets

Les Halles

worry-about-size gifts. You will find a wide selection in the department stores, especially at *Au Printemps* and *Samaritaine de Luxe* as well as in these outstanding houses:

> *La Grande Maison de Blanc,* 8 Place de l'Opéra. Famous large store that also stocks lingerie and clothes for women and girls.
>
> *Noel,* 90 Rue La Boétie.

Lingerie. French handmade lingerie, especially with hand embroidery, is still the finest in the world.

> *A La Ville du Puy,* 36 Rue Tronchet. Exclusively designed blouses, linens, and baby clothes, as well as lingerie.
>
> *Pache,* 6 Rue Castiglione. Good quality at fair prices.
>
> *Benoit Lascoumes,* 33 Rue Godot-deMauroy. Tops in exquisite lingerie.
>
> *Eres,* 2 Rue Tronchet. Large variety of lingerie and fashionable "at-homewear."

Men's Wear. Paris is becoming almost as famous as London for men's clothes, and it also has excellent accessories, especially gloves, hats, shirts, and leather goods.

> *Carnaval de Venise,* 3 Boulevard de la Madeleine.
>
> *Charvet,* 8 Place Vendôme. Famous for ties and shirts.
>
> *Silvers,* 8 Rue Boudreau. Custom-made ties. Fine socks.
>
> *Dominique France,* 58 Rue Pierre Charron. Handmade ties of original design.
>
> *Pierre Faivret,* 165 St. Honoré.
>
> *Larsen,* 346 Rue St. Honoré. Tops for hats and gloves.
>
> *Madelios,* 10 Place de la Madeleine. First-class, handy department store for everything for men.

Moment of decision—wine tasting

Perfumes. Perfumes are, of course, perhaps the best buy of all. But many French perfumes bear trademarks registered in the United States and of these only one bottle in each scent may be taken back. Check with the shop where you buy. If you send perfume directly to someone in the U.S. marked "gift, less than $10.00," there are no customs restrictions. Perfumes may be purchased in any number of stores, including the special export shops mentioned earlier. However, you may enjoy a visit to the elegant shops of the famous French perfume houses. Only the most popular are listed here.

Balmain, 44 Rue François Ier.
Caron, 10 Place Vendôme.
Carven, 6 Rond-Point des Champs-Elysées.
Chanel, 31 Rue Cambon.
Christian Dior, 13 Rue François Ier.
Guerlain, 2 Place Vendôme and 68 Champs-Elysées.
Lancôme, 29 Rue du Faubourg St. Honoré.
Lanvin, 22 Rue du Faubourg St. Honoré.
Molyneux, 5 Rue Royale.
Patou, 7 Rue St. Florentin.
Revillon, 42 Rue de la Boétie.
Rochas, 33 Rue François I.
Roger et Gallet, 62 Rue du Faubourg St. Honoré.
Schiaparelli, 21 Place Vendôme.
Weil, 15 Rue Cortambert.

Umbrellas. French umbrellas are a good buy because they are not only chic but exceptionally well made. Travelers will cherish those with handles that unscrew for packing. All the department stores have good selections.

> *Madeleine Gély*, 218 Blvd. St. Germain.
> *Vedrenne*, 9 Rue St. Roch. Most famous umbrella house in France. Makes the elegant umbrellas for couturiers.

Wines and Liqueurs. If you wish to exceed the quart of spirits allowed duty free, there is no better place for wine than Paris. Those who stay within the quart limit usually pick fine brandies and liqueurs, or perhaps a vintage champagne, because these represent the most savings. The firms listed here have large selections and are expert at packing and shipping things for export.

> *Corcellet*, 18 Avenue de l'Opéra.
> *Comestibles Duñau*, 32 Blvd. Haussman.
> *Fauchon*, 26 Place de la Madeleine.

Chain Stores. In addition to the many specialized shops noted in this chapter, there are three chains of stores that may intrigue visitors to Paris.

One is PRISUNIC with 100 branches in and around Paris. A handy one for visitors is in the Champs-Elysées district at 109 Rue La Boétie, 8e.

The second is MONOPRIX, also a very large chain, with an easily accessible branch at 95 Rue de Provence, 9e.

Both are good examples of the way American mass retailing methods are invading France, long a stronghold of small, highly personal shops. PRISUNIC and MONOPRIX will remind many of the Woolworth chain in the United States.

The third Parisian chain has at present only three stores, but each is enormous and fascinating. This chain is operated on a somewhat more ambitious level than the other two, in certain respects. It is called INNO-FRANCE and offers an eye-popping variety of products from the Common Market countries, the United States, Japan and elsewhere. The most easily accessible branch is located at 35 Rue du Départ in Montparnasse.

Virtually all branches of all three chains have food super markets and in nearly all of them you can buy anything from blue jeans to inexpensive women's dresses to bedroom slippers to bicycles to frozen fish (some of which comes from Scandinavia).

CHAPTER *8*

There is so much to do and see in Paris itself that most casual tourists don't save enough time to explore the outskirts of the capital. This is a pity, because Paris lies in the province of *Ile de France,* the ancient heartland of France and one of the most fascinating and beautiful regions in the whole country. There is an incredible profusion of history-entwined castles, superb cathedrals, art treasures, and country pleasures to be enjoyed within a small radius of the city. At the very least, don't miss the unique experience of Versailles and Chartres.

Green forests surround Paris like a giant park, and the open country is almost immediately accessible. With the exception of Chartres, which is sixty miles away, any of the excursions listed here can be done in a morning or afternoon. Guided tours by American Express and other large travel agencies are made daily to all of these places. But if you prefer to travel at your own pace, they are very easily reached by car, train, or bus. (Routes preceded by the letter N are national highways.) If you dislike crowds, you won't, of course, go on Saturdays or Sundays. Remember, however, that many places of interest are closed on Tuesdays.

VERSAILLES

Thirteen miles west of Paris by car. Leave by Porte St. Cloud and take Route N 10 or take the Autoroute de l'ouest. Train at either Gare St. Lazare or Gare Montparnasse, bus from the Pont de Sèvres stop.

When he was only twenty-three years old, Louis XIV decided to build a glorious new setting for his royal court, which would outshine anything owned by the great nobles of France—and would not be as uncomfortably close to the Paris mobs as the Louvre Palace. The palace and gardens of Versailles turned out to be the most sumptuous court setting the world has ever known, and the inspiration for all royal palaces ever after. There were thick forests and marshes around the chosen site so that leveling and draining the ground proved to be a prodigious project; the extravagant splendor of the gardens took more than fifty years to perfect. But about twenty years after the work was first started, most of the gardens and the main palace, complete with its own chapel, were finished. In 1682 the king and his entire royal court, consisting of some twenty thousand people, moved to Versailles to live in a fantastic private world of their own.

The Palace. If you use the main entrance, the *Place d'Armes* (where cars are parked), your first view of the palace may be disappointing. Because this is a rather bare and cobblestoned esplanade, and because the side of the palace seen from here is spoiled by two wings added in the 18th century. By far the best view is from the opposite garden side where you get the magnificent effect of the unbroken horizontal lines of the wide classic facade.

Since the interior is immense, it is probably fortunate that the only way it can be seen is by a guided tour. Unless you are with a special party, your guide will give his spiel in French; but he almost always speaks very slowly and distinctly, with long pauses between sentences. If you have had any high-school French, you ought to be able to understand most of what he says. Take special note of such highlights as: the *King's State Apartments,* which include the dazzling Hall of Mirrors; the reception rooms with their profusion of sculpture, painted ceilings, and munificent decorations; the *Petits Appartements,* where the king and queen actually lived; the beautiful *Chapel* by Mansart; and the miniature gem-like *Opera House* designed by Gabriel. Everything here reflects the glory of *Le Roi Soleil,* the Sun King, and every room has a painting or statue of him.

The most famous room is the *Galerie des Glaces* (Hall of Mirrors), one of the longest (235 feet) and most elegant in the world. This masterpiece of the classic Louis XIV style is crammed with historical associations. At the time of the Franco-Prussian War, it was the headquarters for the German Army, and in 1871, the King of Prussia was proclaimed Emperor of Germany here. In 1919 it was the happier scene of the signing of the Treaty of Versailles by a defeated Germany. From its wide windows there is a wonderful view of the gardens, which are also reflected in the mirrored wall.

During the Revolution the palace was sacked by a mob from Paris, led by those robust women, the stall-keepers of Les Halles, who marched on Versailles, murdered the bodyguard of Louis XVI,

Versailles is a spectacle—a wonder

and hauled the king and his family to Paris. They also destroyed much of the furniture. Through the generosity of John D. Rockefeller, Jr., and other Americans, however, many of the Royal Suites have been restored and are now open to the public.

The Gardens. If the interior of Versailles is impressive, the fabulous gardens are even more so. They are the work of Le Nôtre, the great garden artist who also designed the Tuileries. The last word in classic French landscaping, they are opulent with beautifully planned vistas, geometrical flower beds, statue-lined walks, broad sweep of lawns and terraces broken by great trees, ornamented lakes, and canals, and, above all, the most magnificent fountains in the world, 1400 of them.

A complete exploration of these 250 acres would take more than three hours. Unless you can give that much time or plan to come back again, it is better to limit yourself to some of the outstanding features, among them: the *Tapis Vert,* the immense green carpet of central lawn; the *Bassin de Neptune,* the largest and one of the most magnificent of the fountain-basins; the *Allée d'Eau,* which has twenty-two small fountains surrounded by charming bronze groups of children; the *Bassin d'Apollon,* with Apollo's spectacular chariot rising from the water; the *Jardin du Roi,* the lovely personal garden of Louis XIV; and especially the *Trianons,* the two miniature palaces which are among the most delightful spots in Versailles.

The Grand Trianon. This beautiful little pink marble building was designed by Mansart for Louis XIV as an informal retreat where he could entertain privately, away from the strict etiquette and pomp of the palace court. It is nearly a mile and a half from the palace. Napoleon was fond of the place too, and stayed here often. The rooms have kept their Louis XIV decorations though the furniture is mostly from Napoleon's time. The romantic little park around it is full of pink flowers.

The French love their national monuments—none better than Versailles

The Petit Trianon was built by Gabriel (designer of the Place de la Concorde) in 1768 for Louis XV. The king spent much of his time in this charming house, first in the company of Mme. de Pompadour and then of Mme. du Barry. When Louis XVI later gave it to Marie Antoinette, it became her favorite residence. Most of the furnishings you see there belonged to the queen; the place has a delicate, graceful, and rather feminine air. The informal garden of this little Trianon was made for Marie Antoinette in the "natural" English style. Open 2–5 P.M. (6 P.M. in summer) except Tuesdays.

Behind the Petit Trianon, built around a large lake, is the Queen's *Hameau,* or Hamlet, a group of little farmhouses where Marie Antoinette and her ladies played at being shepherdesses, industriously churning their butter in the dairy and tending their perfumed sheep. As you walk through these gardens, you will notice many other little buildings and pavilions. One of the most beautifully proportioned is the *Pavillon Français,* which was used for royal picnics.

The fountains. A most breath-taking sight in Versailles is the great fountains which play every afternoon and are illuminated twice a year in summer. There are also special shows with lights and music, tableaux, and ballets that take place nearly every evening during the summer.

Restaurants. *Hôtel Trianon Palace*, 1 Blvd. de la Reine (950 34–12). Lovely garden and outstanding cuisine. Expensive. *Brasserie de l'Ile de France,* 45 Rue Carnot (950 05–28). Moderate. *Londres,* 7 Rue Colbert (950 05–79). Moderate. *Chapeau-Gris,* 7 Rue Hoche (950 10–81). Inexpensive. *La Flotille,* Allée des Matelots. Lunch only. Situated in the park. Closed Dec., Jan., and Feb. Inexpensive.

LA MALMAISON

Ten miles west of Paris by car. Leave from Porte de Neuilly and take Route N 13. Train from Gare St. Lazare, bus from Pont de Neuilly. Train and bus terminals are in the town of Rueil, about 1½ miles from Malmaison.

Both Malmaison and St. Germain-en-Laye, reached by the same auto, train, or bus routes, can be comfortably seen in one morning or afternoon. Unlike most of the châteaux around Paris, *La Malmai-*

son is not at all palace-like, but rather a simple and charming country house that evokes more sentimental memories of Napoleon and Josephine than any other place. Josephine had bought it, and here in these informal rustic surroundings General Bonaparte courted her, and here they spent the early happiest years of their married life. After the annulment of their heirless marriage, the ex-Empress retired to Malmaison. On the first anniversary of her death, Napoleon made a sentimental visit to their old home, just a few days before he left for St. Helena.

The rooms have been authentically decorated with the furniture, clothing, and personal belongings (gathered from many places besides Malmaison) of Napoleon and Josephine. On the ground floor you may see, among a host of other things, the coronation robes of the Emperor, his camp furniture, mapping instruments, notebooks, and the desk where he drafted the *Code Napoléon.* There is also an interesting display of the gowns and jewels of the Empress. The private apartments are rich in personal mementos, including the bedroom screen embroidered by Josephine, many family portraits, Napoleon's camp bed from St. Helena, and their death masks. The little park around the house is noted for its lovely garden, to which Josephine had devoted herself after she retired to Malmaison. It is still planted with the same variety of roses.

Restaurants. (At Rueil-Malmaison): *Auberge du Fruit Défendu,* 3 Quai Halage (967 14–92). Terrace on the Seine. Expensive. Closed Sun. evening and Mon. *El Chiquito,* 126 Avenue Paul Doumer (967 00–53). Closed Sundays and August. Patio. Expensive. (At Bougival): *Le Coq Hardi,* 16 Quai Rennequin-Sualem (969 01–43). Closed Wednesdays and in January. Open noon to 4 and 7 to 10 P.M. The most sumptuous inn around Paris. Expensive.

ST. GERMAIN-EN-LAYE

Fourteen miles from Paris by car. Leave from Porte de Neuilly and take Route N 13. Train from Gare St. Lazare, bus from the Pont de Neuilly. R.E.R. (express métro) from Charles de Gaulle or Auber métro stations.

The first château at St. Germain-en-Laye was a fortress-castle built at the edge of ten thousand acres of royal hunting grounds by Louis VI (the Fat) in the 12th century. The 16th-century castle you see today, which was almost completely rebuilt by François I, still bears the austere look of a medieval fortress. Until Versailles was completed, it was one of the main seats of the French court (Louis XIV was born here), and it also housed some stray English royalty. Mary Stuart lived here from the age of six until sixteen, when she was married to her childhood friend the Dauphin; after Charles I was beheaded, his widow found refuge here; and James II ended his days at St. Germain after his exile from England.

The main things to see in the castle are the chapel, the ballroom.

and the museum. The *Sainte-Chapelle* was built by Saint Louis (Louis IX) in the early part of the 13th century. Especially interesting are its carved figures of St. Louis and his family, the oldest actual portraits of a French royal family. It was in the majestic double-storied ballroom, called *Salle de Mars* (because it was originally a guard room) that Louis XIV held his great receptions and Molière and his theatrical company performed their comedies. The *Musée d'Antiquités Nationales,* (open daily except Tuesdays), is a unique museum with a wonderful collection of prehistoric and Gallo-Roman art objects (the gold and bronze jewelry of pre-Roman times is particularly beautiful), as well as exhibitions reconstructing life in ancient France.

The chief attraction of St. Germain-en-Laye, however, is not the castle, but its setting: the magnificent forests, a popular holiday spot for Parisians; the delightful gardens laid out by Le Nôtre, this time in the English informal style; and above all, the two vast terraces. The *Petite Terrasse* is impressive enough, but the *Grande Terrasse* is one of the most unforgettable sights around Paris. Lined with century-old lime trees, it stretches for a mile and a half in front of the castle and commands a panorama of the Seine Valley all the way to Paris.

Restaurants. *Pavillon Henri IV,* 21 Rue Thiers (963–20–66). Really luxurious. Set at edge of park, with large terrace giving magnificent view of the Seine River and Paris. Closed Jan. and Feb. Expensive. *Cazaudehore,* Avenue President Kennedy (963 08–93). Good food in pleasant flower garden set in forest. Expensive. *Ermitage des Loges,* 11 Ave. Loges (963 04–35). Expensive. Swimming pool. *Pavillon d'Estrées,* 1 Rue Arcades (963 20–83). Good food at moderate prices. *Le Trouvère,* 53 Rue Paris (963 12–23). Inexpensive.

CHARTRES

> *Sixty miles from Paris by car. Take Autoroute A 11 from the Pont de Sèvres directly to Chartres. Train from Gare Montparnasse.*

Everything about Chartres is delightful. The first delightful surprise is to find such a magnificent cathedral in such a small place. The town of Chartres has remained a typical provincial French city, with hilly narrow streets and gabled little houses. Typical except that it contains the loveliest Gothic cathedral in France, perhaps in all of Europe. The present Cathedral of *Notre Dame de Chartres* was begun in 1194 after a fire had destroyed most of the previous church, except the towers, the crypt, and some of the stained glass. It was completed in the remarkably short space of thirty years.

The best way to approach Chartres is on the road from Ablis.

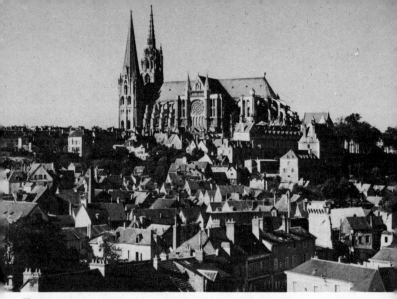

Chartres

Long before the town comes into view, you can see the cathedral's majestic towers rising in the distance, as if right out of the golden wheat fields. In the square in front of the cathedral, you are struck by the lack of symmetry, yet perfect balance, of the two dissimilar towers. The *New Tower*, which dates from 1134, is really the older. It is called new because its ornamental spire was added in the 16th century. The so-called *Old Tower* has been left untouched and is pure Romanesque.

All the doorways are extraordinary, but the *Royal Portal,* in the center of the main façade, is one of the finest pieces of religious art anywhere. The elongated figures of the statues, with their drapery exquisitely designed to blend with the upsweeping slender lines of the doorway, produce a mystical effect. Notice how the intensely expressive faces contrast with their stylized bodies. The small figures on which the main statues rest and the wealth of other little carvings are so delightfully animated and fanciful that they beg for another visit to explore them.

As you enter the cathedral, your first sight of the jewelled light of the stained glass will give new meaning to that phrase "an unforgettable experience." The windows of Chartres, the most complete that have come down to us from the 12th and 13th centuries, are the most beautiful in the world. Their incredible brilliance is high-lighted by an intense clear blue, the famous—and never duplicated—"Chartres blue." If one has to choose among such beauty, the three windows of the main façade—the window on the south side known as *Notre Dame de la Belle Verrière* (Virgin of the Beautiful Window), and the two rose windows—are generally considered the finest. In the south arm of the transept is a large window depicting the life of

St. Fulbert, called the *American Window* because it was presented in 1954 by the Association of American Architects.

When you have seen the windows, note the superb vaulting of the Gothic nave (wider than any other French cathedral), the graceful columns, and the extraordinary harmony of line and proportion everywhere. The maze in the middle of the nave is one of those rare church mazes still intact, where the faithful used to cover its winding passages on their knees. Among the other high points are the exquisitely fashioned Renaissance choir screen; the *Virgin of the Pillar,* an old and much venerated wooden statue; the lovely Pyat and Vendôme chapels; and the ancient crypt, the largest in France. In back of the cathedral you will find the graceful pierced flying buttresses, and the Bishopric Gardens overlooking the old houses and bridges of the Eure River.

Most people, once they have seen a cathedral, do not go back. But Chartres is the kind of place that will make you want to return. For one thing, the stained glass looks completely different in the afternoon than in the morning; the windows seem to change with the sun from hour to hour. There are many people who never fail to go to Chartres every time they come to Paris; always they find it a rewarding experience.

Restaurants. *Hôtel du Grand Monarque,* 22 Place Epars (21 00–72). Moderate. *Hôtel de France,* 10 Place Epars (21 00–07). Moderate. *Vieille Maison,* 5 Rue au Lait (21 10–67). Exceptional food with regional specialties. Closed Mondays and June 15 to July 10. Moderate. *Cazalis,* 31 Rue Soleil d'Or (21 01–55). Closed Mon. evening and Tues., also for two weeks in Feb. and July. Moderate. *Normand,* 24 Place Epars (21 04–38). Inexpensive. *Macé,* 24 Rue Noël-Ballay (21 34–10). Inexpensive.

ST. DENIS

Seven miles north of Paris by car. Leave from Porte de la Chapelle and take Route N 1 directly to St. Denis or take the Autoroute du Nord A 1. Train from the Gare du Nord, bus from Porte de la Chapelle or Porte de Clignancourt.

The basilica of St. Denis stands in the center of a particularly unattractive industrial suburb of Paris that would hardly merit a visit merely to see another fine Gothic church. But St. Denis, where the kings of France were crowned and buried, offers a unique panorama of the history of France through the sculptures of its royal tombs. The original basilica was built in the 5th century over the spot where the martyred St. Denis, patron saint of France, was supposed to have fallen after he had walked from Paris with his severed head in his hand. The present building, begun in the early 12th, and enlarged in the 13th century, suffered great destruction during the Revolution and has been much restored (fortunately or unfortunately according to your taste). It was at St. Denis that Henri IV was barred from en-

tering Paris until, standing in the church entrance, he solemnly re-
nounced Protestantism (for the second time), with the remark that
"Paris is well worth a mass."

When St. Louis (Louis IX) chose this church in the early 13th century to be the royal burial place, he ordered tombs to be made of all
French royalty back to the first King Dagobert. Most of the statues
for these tombs were made from portraits, and they are the only like-
nesses we have of these early kings. Louis' son Philip III (the Bold)
started the practice of having the faces sculptured from the actual
death masks, and these are even more authentic portraits. The many
monuments that make St. Denis a real museum of French royalty
are far too numerous to mention here, but the following are of outstanding historical and artistic interest: *Dagobert I,* the tomb of the
earliest king of France is especially interesting for the reliefs showing
the torment and redemption of Dagobert's soul; *St. Louis and his
family*—these 13th-century effigies have a rare grace and dignity;
Louis XII and Anne of Brittany—a beautifully designed tomb with
expressive figures of the royal pair was done by the Italian sculptor
Giovanni di Giusto (Jean Juste); *François I*—one of the best works
of Philibert Delorme, shows the king kneeling by the side of his wife
and three children; *Henri II and Catherine de' Medici*—this double
tomb of Henri II and his wife, perhaps the most beautiful here, is by
Germain Pilon, one of the finest sculptors of the French Renaissance.

Restaurant. (St. Denis does not have good restaurants. You will do
better in Chantilly or Paris.) *Grill St. Denis*, 59 Rue de Strasbourg
(752 61–98). Closed Sundays. Moderately priced.

CHANTILLY

> *Twenty-five miles from Paris by car. Leave from Porte de la
> Chapelle and take Route N 1 through St. Denis until it meets
> N 16 going directly into Chantilly. Train from Gare du Nord.*

The pleasant resort town of Chantilly is famous for its race track—
the French Derby is run here every summer—and the château with its

Chantilly

Hall of Mirrors—Versailles

superb art collection. Chantilly has been a racing center for a long time, and the amazingly luxurious 18th-century stone stables (with stalls for 250 horses and 400 hounds, and rooms for huntsmen, grooms, etc.), form an interesting side light on French architecture. Handsomely designed with fine doorway carvings, they look more like a palace than a stable.

The château itself has been drastically restored and is now perhaps too elaborate, but its setting couldn't be improved upon. Perched high on a hill rising out of a lake, and surrounded by lovely gardens and a deep mysterious forest, it looks like an enchanted fairy-tale palace. This Renaissance château was the country home of the noble and illustrious Condé family, and when the last descendant, the Duc d'Aumale, built an additional building to house his immense collection of paintings, it turned out to be even larger than the original château. Incidentally, it was at Chantilly that the famous chef Vatel committed suicide during a dinner for Louis XIV, because, it is said, the fish failed to arrive in time.

The Duc d'Aumale left his magnificent collection to France on the condition that the paintings should never be removed from Chantilly or lent for any exhibition. (If you go to see the art treasures here, make sure that there are no races scheduled because the castle is closed on those days.) The collection is uniquely rich in French paintings and illuminations of the 15th and 16th centuries, especially in the drawings and portraits of Jean and François Clouet. *Les Très Riches Heures du Duc de Berri,* one of the most famous illuminated manuscripts in the world, illustrates the months of the year. There are also many works by such masters as Giotto, Botticelli, Raphael, Memling, Van Dyck, Fouquet, and Poussin. If you don't have time to see all the rooms, go first to the little one called the Sanctuary, which contains some of the chief artistic treasures of the whole collection. Here you will find Raphael's lovely *Madonna of the House of Orleans* and *The Three Graces;* between them is the extraordinary marriage-chest panel by Filippino Lippi. Here, too, are forty exquisite miniature paintings by the early French master, Jean Fouquet.

Restaurants. *Relais Condé,* 42 Ave. du Maréchal Joffre (457 05–75). Closed Mon. evenings, Tuesdays and August. Moderate prices. *Chantilly Bar,* 9 Ave. du Général Leclerc (457 04–65). Closed

Fridays and March. Simple, delicious, inexpensive. *Relais du Coq-Chantant*, 21 Route Creil (457 01–28). Closed Thursdays and February. Moderate. *Tipperary*, 6 Ave. du Maréchal Joffre (457 00–48). Closed Wednesdays and February. Good food, moderate prices.

FONTAINEBLEAU

Thirty-six miles south of Paris by car. Take Autoroute du Sud A 6 from Porte d'Orléans or Porte d'Italie, or leave by Porte d'Italie and take Route N 7 directly to Fontainebleau. Train from Gare de Lyon.

You approach the *Château Fontainebleau* through one of the most extensive forests in France. From the 12th through the 16th centuries, this was the favorite hunting ground for French kings, and first a hunting lodge, then a royal fortress, stood where the elaborate castle stands today. In 1528 François I decided to rebuild Fontainebleau completely, and the oldest part of the present château dates from that period. Its rather Italian air is not accidental; François I was a great admirer of the Italian Renaissance and imported a large group of Florentine (including Benvenuto Cellini) and Roman artists to work for him. The castle became the favorite residence of many French kings, and innumerable changes and modifications and new wings and other additions were made by them. Every king and every period left an imprint on Fontainebleau, and the conglomeration of many-styled buildings that make up the present palace has been described as a "rendez-vous des châteaux," and by Napoleon as "la Maison des Siècles"—the House of Centuries.

Fontainebleau is replete with romantic history: many French kings were born and died here; foreign royalty came to visit; and the many court favorites, such as Diane de Poitiers and Gabrielle d'Estrées, inspired much of the rebuilding. But above all, Fontainebleau recalls Napoleon, who preferred it to Versailles, perhaps because the latter was so dedicated to the glory of Louis XIV. One of Napoleon's illustrious visitors was Pope Pius VII, who came in 1804 to crown him as

Fontainbleau

Emperor. For the Pope's second visit, he was abducted from Rome and kept a virtual prisoner for eighteen months until he had been browbeaten first into granting his consent to the annulment of Napoleon's marriage to Josephine, and then (in 1812) into signing an agreement renouncing all his temporal power (which he later repudiated). Just two years later, Napoleon abdicated his own power at Fontainebleau. The main courtyard which used to be known as the *Cour de Cheval Blanc* (White Horse) is now generally called the *Cour des Adieux,* since it was here that Napoleon took his touching farewell of his faithful Old Guard, just before his exile to Elba. This scene of the Emperor standing on the graceful horseshoe-shaped stairway and reviewing his troops for the last time has been dramatically rendered by many painters and writers.

Among the other noteworthy sights around the château are the *Bassin des Carpes,* renowned for its gigantic carp, reported to be hundreds of years old; the *Jardin de Diane* with its bronze fountain-statue of Diana; the beautiful formal gardens by Le Nôtre and the naturalistic garden of Napoleon; the Chinese Museum; and an ancient grape trellis, known as the *Treille du Roi,* which was planted at the time of Louis XIV and still yields excellent white grapes for wine.

The Interior. Frequent guided tours go through the State Apartments on the ground floor where the two finest rooms are the *Galerie François I,* with its beautiful Renaissance decorations and frescos by Italian artists, and the *Galerie Henri II* (sometimes called "The Ballroom") with its handsome ceiling and everywhere the bow-and-arrow, the crescent-moon emblems, and the King's initial intertwined with "D," for his mistress, Diane de Poitiers. The *Apartments of Napoleon I* give a revealing picture of how he lived after he became emperor and are crammed with Napoleonic mementos, including his

Gate House at Fontainebleau

Great Hall at Fontainebleau

special clock with ten dials, the little table on which he wrote his abdication, and in his bedroom, the royal bed, with the cradle of his infant son beside it.

Intensely interesting as the château is, the chief glory of Fontainebleau is undoubtedly its immense (50,000 acres) wild and romantic forest, the most beautiful in France. The unique nature of the soil and sub-soil here and much erosion have developed an incredible variety of sandy heaths, romantic areas of huge rocks, breath-taking gorges with rushing torrents between them, and noble old trees, some of them twenty-four feet in diameter. The wild grandeur of this forest made it the favorite painting place for Millet, Rousseau, Daumier, Corot, and other landscape artists from nearby Barbizon. Two of the most famous of the rocky wilderness gorges are the *Gorges d'Apremont* and the *Gorges de Franchard,* the latter the scene of Robert Louis Stevenson's "The Treasure of Franchard." Today the forest of Fontainebleau is the most popular weekend camping site for the boy scouts and young men of Paris. For more casual and less rugged visitors, there is a great variety of scenic drives and pleasant walks that go to all the picturesque spots in the forest.

Restaurants. *Grand Veneur,* on Route N 7 in nearby Barbizon (437 40–44). Pleasant rustic dining room with very good food and fine view of the forest. Closed Wed. and August. Expensive. *Hôtel de l'Aigle Noir,* 27 Place Napoleon Bonaparte (422 20–27). Moderately expensive. *Filet de Sole,* 5 Rue du Coq-Gris (422 25–05). Near the palace. Closed Tues. evening, Wed. and July. Moderately expensive. *Chez Arrighi,* 53 Rue de France (422 29–43). Closed Sunday nights, Mondays, and July. Tables in garden under trees. Moderate. *Franchard,* in middle of Fountainebleau Forest, near the spectacular Franchard Gorge (422 29–69). Closed Mon. evenings and Tuesdays. Moderate.

125

126

127

K E Y   T O   P A R I S

● POINTS OF INTEREST   ○ RAILWAY STATIONS

1 ARC DE TRIOMPHE
2 MUSEUM OF MODERN ART
3 PALAIS DE CHAILLOT
4 EIFFEL TOWER
5 ECOLE MILITAIRE
6 LES INVALIDES
7 PALAIS BOURBON
8 PLACE DE LA CONCORDE
9 LA MADELEINE
10 THE OPERA HOUSE
11 AMERICAN EXPRESS
12 JARDIN DES TUILERIES
13 THE LOUVRE

14 COLONNE VENDOME
15 COMEDIE FRANÇAIS
16 PALAIS-ROYAL
17 ST. GERMAIN DES PRES
18 SAINTE CHAPELLE
19 CONCIERGERIE
20 PALAIS DE JUSTICE
21 NOTRE DAME
22 HOTEL DE VILLE
23 JARDIN DU LUXEMBOURG
24 PALAIS DU LUXEMBOURG
25 AMERICAN EMBASSY
26 PANTHEON